BIBLE STUDY COMMENTARY

Ezra-Job

Bible Study Commentary

Ezra–Job

P. SOUTHWELL

130 City Road, London EC1V 2NJ

Fort Washington, Pennsylvania 19034

© 1982 Scripture Union
130 City Road, London EC1V 2NJ

First published 1982

ISBN 0 86201 114 0 (UK)
      0 87508 156 8 (USA)

Maps: Jenny Grayston

Phototypeset in Great Britain by
Input Typesetting Ltd., London SW19 8DR.

Printed in Great Britain by
Ebenezer Baylis & Son Limited
The Trinity Press, Worcester, and London.

General Introduction

The worldwide church in the last quarter of the twentieth century faces a number of challenges. In some places the church is growing rapidly and the pressing need is for an adequately trained leadership. Some Christians face persecution and need support and encouragement while others struggle with the inroads of apathy and secularism. We must come to terms, too, with the challenges presented by Marxism, Humanism, a belief that 'science' can conquer all the ills of mankind, and a whole range of Eastern religions and modern sects. If we are to make anything of this confused and confusing world it demands a faith which is solidly biblical.

Individual Christians, too, in their personal lives face a whole range of different needs – emotional, physical, psychological, mental. As we think more and more about our relationships with one another in the body of Christ and as we explore our various ministries in that body, as we discover new dimensions in worship and as we work at what it means to embody Christ in a fallen world we need a solid base. And that base can only come through a relationship with Jesus Christ which is firmly founded on biblical truth.

The Bible, however, is not a magical book. It is not enough to say, 'I believe', and quote a few texts selected at random. We must be prepared to work with the text until our whole outlook is moulded by it. We must be ready to question our existing position and ask the true meaning of the word for us in our situation. All this demands careful study not only of the text but also of its background and of our culture. Above all it demands prayerful and expectant looking to the Spirit of God to bring the word home creatively to our own hearts and lives.

This new series of books has been commissioned in response to the repeated requests for something new to follow on from Bible Characters and Doctrines. It is now over ten years since the first series of Bible Study Books was produced and it is hoped the new series will reflect the changes of the last ten years and bring the Bible text to life for a new generation of readers. The series has three aims:

1. To encourage regular, systematic, personal Bible reading. Each volume is divided into sections ideally suited to daily use, and will normally provide material for three months (the exceptions being Psalms and 1 Corinthians-Galatians, four months, and Mark and Ezra-Job, two months). Used in this way the books will cover the entire Bible in five years. The comments aim to give background information and enlarge on the meaning of the text, with special reference to the contemporary relevance. Detailed questions of application are, however, often left to the reader. The questions for further study are designed to aid in this respect.

2. To provide a resource manual for group study. These books do not provide a detailed plan for week by week study. Nor do they present a group leader with a complete set of ready-made questions or activity ideas. They do, however, provide the basic biblical material and, in the questions for further discussion, they give starting points for group discussion.

3. To build into a complete Bible commentary. There is, of course, no shortage of commentaries. Here, however, we have a difference. Rather than look at the text verse by verse the writers examine larger blocks of text, preserving the natural flow of the original thought and observing natural breaks.

Writers have based their comments on the RSV and some have also used the New International Version in some detail. The books can, however, be used with any version.

Introduction

The books of Ezra and Nehemiah contain miscellaneous material, dating from the century after Israel's return from exile in Babylon. The major component is the memoirs of Nehemiah, governor of Judah from 445/4 BC onwards, but there are a few chapters about Ezra, whom the Persian emperor Artaxerxes had sent to order the worship of Israel's God in the Temple, and to re-establish observance of God's law. In addition some letters and decrees of successive Persian rulers which pertain to Jewish affairs are cited, in the kind of Aramaic used in official correspondence in those days. The final publication of these texts was probably in the early fourth century BC shortly after the events to which they refer. It is unlikely that their editing was the work of the author of Chronicles, as some believe, nor is the evidence for another popular theory, namely that Nehemiah's ministry preceded Ezra's, as compelling as many have thought. Be that as it may, our interest will be primarily with what these books tell us about God and his dealings with his people. Apparently forsaken by him in Babylon, apparently deceived by false prophets of hope (see Jer. 14:13, 14), and apparently beyond political recovery, there was much work of reconstruction to be done, not only politically, but in their hearts. It was also to be a period marked by two comparatively new phenomena in Israel. First, Judaism was now an international religion. God has pushed his reluctant witnesses out into the world they were called to serve. Thus more Jews lived outside Judah than in it, and soon more spoke other tongues than those who spoke Hebrew. The Dispersion had begun. The other novelty was sectarian rivalry within Judah itself, and the long and painful emergence of the group centred around Shechem who were later to become the Samaritan sect is one of the sadder features of Israel's post-exilic history. The beginnings of the affair lie within the period covered by these books.

Analysis of Ezra

1:1–2:63 A fresh start

In 587 BC Jerusalem fell to Nebuchadnezzar's Babylonian troops and their Edomite allies. So the prophetic words of Jeremiah were finally vindicated. The exiled Daniel (9:2) studied that prophet's letter to the Jewish exiles (Jer. 29:1–28) to see when the captivity might end, and in our opening verse here further vindication of Jeremiah is found, in Cyrus the Persian's decree (2–4, compare 2 Chron. 36:23) that the Jews might return to their homeland, and to their ancestral ways of worship, in about 539 BC. The seventy years were fulfilled. God had remembered his people, as in Egypt long ago.

Two incidental consequences of this were, first, that Jeremiah's literary remains were collected and edited, together (probably) with those of other prophets, to form the nucleus of a prophetic canon. This paralleled the great historical work, also edited in the exile and shortly after, which runs from Joshua to 2 Kings. What that history illustrated was what the prophets had proclaimed. In the second place, the Jews' experience of false prophecy (see Jer. 23:9–15) led them to a gradual rejection of the prophetic office, a rejection which was powerfully expressed a little later by Zechariah (Zech. 13:2–6). Soon, under Ezra, Judaism was to be a religion of written law rather than prophetic oracle.

Cyrus' decree has survived, inscribed on a contemporary cylinder, using language very similar to that of the Bible, both here, and in Isaiah 45:1–3. Though not a monotheist, he respected the power of foreign gods to give him success and long life. The Babylonian Jews had no images of Yahweh their God, but were able to take back with them some of the treasures plundered from the old Jerusalem Temple (7–11).

It is noteworthy that in all this God's initiative is preserved (he 'stirred up' 1, 5). Neither Cyrus' superstition, nor Jeremiah's prediction, nor the Jews' aspiration was called upon to explain this decree. God alone is Lord, of good things as of evil (Isa. 44:24–28; 45:7). Chapter 2 supplies a list of those who initially chose to return under the otherwise unknown Sheshbazzar, and Zerubbabel, nephew of the last king in Jerusalem (see 1 Chron. 3:19). Few Levites thought the enterprise worthwhile (42), perhaps because of the inferior role they were to play in the post-exilic Temple. Many Jews were comfortable in exile and chose not to seek God in the new Temple (Isa. 55:6–13). However, it is encouraging that all classes of Jewish society were represented in the great trek.

THOUGHT: God alone is Lord.

2:64–3:13 The priority of worship

Though our book bears the name of Ezra, Ezra himself does not feature until chapter 7. Its chief purpose is to record the process by which Jerusalem and the Temple were restored to the glory predicted in Isaiah 54 and Ezekiel 40–48. The pictures those prophets used are metaphorical, but even so the reality fell short of expectations (12), the community being smaller, poorer and less secure than in the days of the Davidic kings. The book of Lamentations expresses, in its acrostic form, the whole gamut, the A to Z, of the wretchedness to which Jerusalem had been brought.

One admires the people of this struggling community for the way they used their time and money. They were generous (68, 69), they observed the feasts and sacrifices demanded by the law (2–6), and were quick to make use of their limited financial resources to get on with the job (7–9).

When the foundations had been laid the event was celebrated in due style (10–13), using the psalm refrain which had been used, according to the Chronicler, at the final dedication of the first Temple (2 Chr. 5:13; 7:3). The uninhibited nature of this noisy celebration was in the spirit of such passages as Isaiah 52:7–10; 42:10. A great deliverance deserves loud proclamation for all to hear. Note how leadership had now passed from Sheshbazzar to the royal Zerubbabel and the priestly Jeshua (2). Both these men were destined to raise the new community's hopes very high.

One of the areas in which Jewish thinking was at this time ambiguous was that of community relations. In verse 7 we find the people happy, as David had been (2 Sam. 5:11) to work with foreigners, an attitude which was to find support later in Malachi (1:11) and Zechariah (8:23), and had already appeared in Isaiah 49:6. But in chapter 4 both native non-Jews and foreign citizens are excluded from the community's most central activities – a foretaste of the future sad prejudices against Gentiles.

QUESTION: A great deliverance deserves loud proclamation – how are we proclaiming our deliverance? Can all hear?

4 Discouraged by opposition

Evidently amongst those who now lived in the environs of Jerusalem were some of the settlers who had been brought to Israel, the northern Hebrew kingdom, by the Assyrians in 721, after their capture of Israel's capital, Samaria (see 2 Kings 17:24–28). These had been taught the religion of Yahweh, but practised their native religions also (2 Kings 17:33). Evidently this settlement policy was a continued one, as Esarhaddon (2) reigned about forty years after Shalmaneser V who attacked Samaria. Their descendants (1–3), together perhaps with Jews who had not been exiled from Judah, now wanted to take their part in the restored cult of Yahweh. They were curtly rebuffed (3) – is there an echo of this in Isaiah 63:15–19? – probably because of the traditional syncretism of their religious practice, and maybe because of their mixed descent. It was important to keep the community undefiled.

Their reaction was petulant (4,5). Neither side came out of this encounter well. The Jews might have recalled that 'a soft answer turns away wrath' (Prov. 15:1), and Christians need to remember this in their doctrinal and denominational quarrels (Jas. 1:19,20). It was a dangerous precedent to appeal to the state for support in an essentially theological dispute (6).

Ahasuerus (6) was probably Xerxes (486–465 BC), and Artaxerxes I reigned from 465–424 (7). But Darius I's second year (24) was 520 BC. Verses 6 to 23 thus refer to later events. Doubtless these excerpts are included here to illustrate the kind of opposition the Jews had to face all along in their attempt to re-fortify Jerusalem. The Temple, however, they did complete in 515 BC, despite the 'adversaries' (6:15). Their reliance on Persian fairness, moreover, was ultimately vindicated by successive decrees of Darius and his successors, of which one is cited here (17–22). But in later times Christians were not as fortunate, as Peter reminds us. Whether or not we deserve our suffering, we have a pattern in Jesus of how to endure it (1 Pet. 2:19–21; 3:9–17; 4:12–19). It would be a mistake, though, to make a facile equivalence between the experience of physical torture, which some must endure, and bureaucratic delaying tactics like those recorded here.

FOR ENCOURAGEMENT: 'Rejoice in so far as you share Christ's sufferings. . . ' (1 Peter 4:13).

5 Prophets – and prefects

One can learn something of the state of the returned exiles from the book of Haggai, the prophet, who, with Zechariah (1), provoked the completion of work on the Temple. According to Haggai (1:2) initial enthusiasm had waned, selfish use of resources had succeeded the earlier generosity (1:4), and poor harvests had led to inflation (1:6) and demoralisation in the face of trouble. Haggai's message was that God had brought this about (1:9–11) because the people were neglecting their religious priorities (Ezra 4:24). When the Temple had been built, prosperity would follow (Hag. 2:6–9), and those who had lamented the earlier building would have no further cause for sorrow. Zerubbabel would then be God's appointed ruler over Jews and Gentiles alike – a messianic figure (Hag. 2:20–23). God's initiative is again seen as he 'stirs up' the people to work (Hag. 1:14). It is often the case that labour becomes a delight when done for God's sake (1 Cor. 15:58; Col. 3:23, 24).

The 'governor of the province Beyond the River' was not a Jew, but a Babylonian (to judge by his name), who had been appointed satrap of that part of the Fertile Crescent west of the Euphrates which stretches from Syria down to the borders of Egypt. Neither he, nor his (apparently) Persian colleague would have much reason to interest themselves in a local temple-building enterprise unless put up to it by the disaffected locals of 4:1. Sheshbazzar's governorship of Palestine had by now, it seems, lapsed (14), and recourse could be had to a higher official. While we cannot approve such childish tactics, we should realize how badly wronged the local people must have felt themselves to be. After all, they had not been punished by exile and they had attempted to preserve the cult of Yahweh all along. They would have had no reason to believe the theology of the new literature of the exilic age (e.g., calling those who had not been exiled 'bad figs', Jer. 24:8–10). Moreover their desire to worship their God with their fellow Jews seems to have been sincere. But instead of understanding, they were met by antagonism, and schism resulted. From the time of Galatians (2:11–14) and Hebrews (10:24, 25; 12:15), Christians have had to make agonising choices between the demands of love and the claims of truth. But even when we differ over truth, we need not be divided in love.

6 The end of the beginning

Persian thoroughness and fairness came to the rescue of the dispirited Jews. The decree of Darius, and the decree of Cyrus incorporated in it, are remarkably similar in form to extra-Biblical documents of the same type. Ezra 4:8–6:18 is in Aramaic, a North-West Semitic tongue, used originally in Damascus, which became a diplomatic language in the Persian Empire (but had been used earlier, see 2 Kings 18:26), and eventually replaced Hebrew as the common tongue of ordinary Jews. These chapters faithfully reflect the Imperial Aramaic style. Darius' own decree also reflects the characteristic cruelty of Persian justice (11). Like Cyrus, Darius desired that the God of the Jews be invoked for himself and his heirs (10). Prayer for secular rulers is a duty laid upon all Christians, too, for Christians believe that the civil power is ordained by God (see Rom. 13:1–7; and 1 Tim. 2:1, 2). As God's 'stirring up' of Cyrus shows, the world's most powerful rulers are not beyond his controlling power.

This section of the book now concludes with the long-awaited climax, twenty-four years after Cyrus' decree, the completion in 515 BC of the new Temple (15). Verse 14 bears witness again to God's initiative behind the actions of two kings. The reference to joy in verses 16 and 22 is all the more notable when compared with the despondency of the previous years: the word joy has not occurred since 3:13.

The Hebrew language is resumed in verse 19 to record what was perhaps by then the most evocative of Jewish feasts: Passover. This festival commemorated the last of the great plagues in Egypt, and the miraculous escape of Israel across the Red Sea (see Exod. 13). At great moments of Israel's history it was through this feast that the people gave emphatic expression to their sense of gratitude to God for new deliverance from foreign tyranny or national apostasy. Examples can be found in 2 Chronicles 30:1–27, and 2 Kings 23:21–23. For Christians the commemoration of Jesus' redeeming death in unbroken observance down the centuries of the Lord's Supper has served a similar purpose (see 1 Cor. 5:7–8). It demonstrates in visual form an outward and visible sign of our redemption, and of God's love for us. The title 'King of Assyria' (22) refers to Darius, King of Persia, whose territories included the area once ruled by the Jews' ancient enemy, Assyria, in defiance of whom Hezekiah's Passover had been observed (compare also Neh. 9:32). Notice also that the Jews were now allowing their native fellow Jews to worship with them (21), so long as their religious practices were orthodox. In the New Testament we are told to put aside party spirit (Phil. 2:1–3; Gal. 5:20).

7 God's second initiative – Ezra

The seventh year of Artaxerxes (7) was 458 BC, so we are now several decades further on in the history of the Jews. There is no good reason to amend this to 'the thirty-seventh year' as some do, to make Ezra more contemporary with Nehemiah. Nor need we suppose that Artaxerxes II is meant, which would reverse the traditional sequence of Ezra and Nehemiah, though the latter proposal enjoys a wide vogue. In 458 Artaxerxes I had only recently suppressed a revolt in Egypt, and it was in his own interests to ensure that Judah was both stable and loyal. Hence the mission of Ezra, whose title (11, 12), though not an official government title, suggests a high degree of royal authority committed to him 'for the house of the God of heaven' (23, compare 27). His mandate was not a secular, civil one (this may explain why Nehemiah later found Jerusalem in such civil disarray, without our having to postulate a later arrival of Ezra after him) but to do with the Temple cult, and with teaching Jewish law (25, 26).

In the former he appears to have been quite successful, though in the latter less so until the work of Nehemiah was well under way (Neh. 8). The decree of Artaxerxes is recorded in contemporary Aramaic (12–26).

We may assume a period of considerable religious laxity in the interval since 515 BC: Malachi testifies to this (1:6–2:4; 13–17; 3:6–15) as does Zechariah (1:1–6). Maybe Ezra had heard of this, for his resolve (10) was to see that God's law (probably the books of Moses, see 6:18) was known and obeyed. His qualifications were obviously considerable, both in ancestry (1–5) and scholarship (6), nor was he averse, as those similarly endowed might be, to undertaking an arduous and potentially dangerous mission for his God. In this respect he is not unlike Paul (compare Phil. 3:4–6). His influence with the Emperor (6) was perhaps not limited to religious affairs in Judah if it was he who provoked a decree ordering Jews in Egypt to keep Passover, and giving instructions on how to observe it (see papyrus 21 from Elephantine dated 419 BC, in the reign of Darius II). His retinue of (presumably) like-minded people (7) would be a blessing on the journey, which was made at a difficult time (8:22), as well as in the work itself. Christians, too, are 'members one of another' (1 Cor. 12) and mutually indispensable. This book is really about a community making a fresh start, not just about one man.

8 Planning a mission

Chapter seven ended with the start of Ezra's own memoirs (27, 28), and now chapters eight and nine continue in the first person. Characteristic of a man who knew the value of team work is the enumeration of those who were to go with him. There was, as before (see 2:40–42) a dearth of Levites, but a delegation consisting both of men in the public eye ('leading men') and 'men of insight' (16) was able to convince a few of the recalcitrants of the high value set by the community upon their service ('ministers for the house of our God' [17]), and to recruit them, suitably attended, into the missionary band – a fine example of Ezra's tact and courtesy, and of his eye for the right men. Casiphia may be Ctesiphon, on the Tigris, where there may have been a Jewish holy place (which is what 'the place' [17] often means) at which the Levites undertook teaching duties, an early form of synagogue, perhaps.

Ezra declined to ask for an armed escort. This was God's work, and was to be undertaken in God's strength alone. Prayer and fasting were the weapons of his warfare (compare Mark 9:29; 2 Cor. 10:4), and at stake was the credibility of the God of Israel in the eyes of Artaxerxes (21–23). At other times in this century the Jews had no such scruples, and the life of Paul provides ample illustration of the variety of choices available to the Christian about invoking one's legal rights and privileges. But there are times when God must be allowed to prove himself. Ezra's faith was rewarded (31).

His faith was, however, matched by his shrewdness, for he took no risks with bad book-keeping (24–30, 34). The treasure, of enormous value, belonged to the Lord, and all of it had to be accounted for. Ezra was aware that he was steward, not master, of all his company conveyed (compare 2 Cor. 8:20, 21).

When the travellers arrived they observed the religious priorities that they had upheld by the river Ahava (21) at the start of the journey. Worship comes before work. Their royal commission having been seen by the local satraps they began to do what lay closest to Ezra's heart, to 'aid the people and the house of God' (35, 36). What had been neglected for decades was now to be repaired. It is noteworthy that this memoir records much planning and preparation (1–36a), and little of the main work (36b). It is often in the planning stage that battles are won and by their modesty that great men are recognised.

QUESTION: Do you allow God to prove himself?

9 A hint of failure

Again some time has elapsed (1, 8), and maybe the task of rectifying the Temple cult had been completed (9). Evidently the task of commending the law of Moses to the Jews had not been so successful (2), a fact of which Ezra was strangely unaware (1, 3). Maybe the Temple and divine service had occupied too much of his time, to the neglect of more pastoral concerns, or perhaps he was one of those great saints of God who simply cannot believe a fellow-worker could be guilty of moral offence. Deuteronomy 7:1–6 had stated in unequivocal terms that Israel's election meant that mixed marriages, i.e. marriages with local non-Jews, were prohibited, because of the danger of apostasy. Verses 11 and 12 of our present chapter are not a quotation from the Bible, but a broad summary of its general stance vis-à-vis such marriages. The Christian is under a similar injunction (e.g. 1 Cor. 7:39; 2 Cor. 6:14). For us, indeed, marriage itself can be viewed as an over-commitment to the world and its affairs (Matt. 19:10–12; 1 Cor. 7:8, 27–35).

The time of the evening sacrifice (4) was a time when Jews, wherever they were, might join in worship or offer prayer (compare Elijah, 1 Kings 18:29; Peter and John, Acts 3:1). Ezra's solitary prayer of penitence thus became a corporate act (4; 10:1, 2). It is a marvellous thing that men as single-minded and holy as Ezra, Nehemiah (1:4–11) and Daniel (9:3–19) could have been so aware of their membership of a sinful community that they could confess the community's sins to God as though they were their own (compare also Isa. 6:5). How much more should Christians accept for themselves the shared guilt of the church and seek God's forgiveness and renewed power for service? Ezra's prayer is full of evidence that he knew the history of the Jewish people well, and the law and the prophets, but above all that he knew God, a God who tolerates no sin amongst those called by his name.

Such knowledge should inform the prayers of all God's people today, especially those of leaders and teachers.

QUESTION: Do we, in our prayer, identify with the surrounding community, or do we like the Pharisees adopt the 'I thank you that I am not as other men' approach?

10 Prayer and repentance

The very act of joining in corporate prayer, it seems, helped create the answer, for no sooner had Ezra finished than the people present were willing to amend their lives according to the law of Moses (1–4). This terrible experience would not lightly be forgotten, and no record survives in the story of what provision was made for the unfortunate victims. In the New Testament divorce is not viewed so lightly, though separation is permitted to a couple of whom only one is a Christian, if the marriage is thereby put under too much strain (1 Cor. 7:15). There is always hope for the unbelieving spouse and the children (1 Cor. 7:14, 16). The gloom of the occasion was intensified by a heavy rainstorm (9), and the whole wretched business dragged on for two months (16, 17). There is no note of rejoicing in this chapter, for even when sin is repented of it often has a sad entail. That is why to 'sin that grace may abound' is not only cynical but foolish (Rom. 6:1–11). A long list of the offenders concludes the book. Their names stand as a memorial to the hopelessness of spiritual compromise. But there was hope for Israel (2): even men's folly can be turned to bring honour to God, and their penitence ensured God's forgiveness.

Jehohanan (6), if he is the same as the Johanan in Nehemiah 12:22, 23, was possibly the grandson of Eliashib who was a contemporary of Nehemiah (3:1). It is important to note, however, that his name is only used to identify the chamber to which Ezra retired, and there is no suggestion that they even met. According to Josephus, his fame came later (after the time of the editing of this book), when he killed his brother Joshua in the Temple precincts.

It is important in this chapter to notice how the national repentance was not only Ezra's work (4), but that of the whole community. When the Spirit of God works, he requires co-operation from God's people as a pre-condition of blessing. A characteristic of the spirit of change Ezra brought was humility (9: compare 8:21), without which God cannot do great things for us. What was true of Mary (Luke 1:38) must be true for us all (1 Peter 5:6).

In many ways Ezra's ministry seemed to have been a failure: Nehemiah after him had to deal with mixed marriages also (13:23–29). But, despite this, many of the ideals he stood for became the hallmarks of later Judaism – for example, the centrality of the Law of Moses, the manner of its interpretation, the primacy of the priesthood, the caution about foreign influences, and the cultic observances of the second Temple. So the discouraging situation in chapter ten is not history's final verdict upon him.

Questions for further study and discussion on Ezra

1. How can we recognise God's initiative in the behaviour of secular authorities (see 1:1)?

2. What were the causes of the hatred and bitterness described in chapters 4 and 5? Are there any ways it could have been avoided?

3. Choose a similar situation in the world today, and pray for all the people involved.

4. 'Christians are mutually indispensable' (see notes on chapter 7). What gifts did the people have who went with Ezra (7:7)? What gifts has God given each member of your own group? How do we discover our gifts and decide how best to use them?

5. When should Christians hedge themselves about with secular support (6:11), and when forego it (8:22)?

6. In the light of chapters 9 and 10, what courses are open to those involved in 'mixed marriages'? What would you recommend to a Christian, and why?

7. What led to the worship and rejoicing of chapter 3? Discuss practical ways in which we can apply these principles in our own lives.

8. How much did Ezra himself achieve, and how much did he inspire in others?

Analysis of Nehemiah

1 God's man for God's moment

The chronicle of the Jewish re-settlement of Judah and Jerusalem now continues with another memoir, that of Nehemiah (1). He has no long ancestry supplied by the editor (contrast Ezra 7:1–5), and we may suppose that he was an ordinary Jewish layman, neither priest nor scholar. His personal qualities, however, had drawn him to the notice of the Persian Emperor, Artaxerxes I, in whose service he was by now cupbearer, an office of considerable prestige. The 'twentieth year' (2:1) was 445 BC, thirteen years after the probable date of the start of Ezra's ministry.

Some time in mid-winter of that year Nehemiah's brother Hanani (see 7:2) brought from Jerusalem the news that the community was in trouble. Maybe this was a reference to the sad events of Ezra 9, 10. Furthermore the city walls, destroyed in 587 BC, had still not been repaired. The attempt referred to in Ezra 4:13,16 had been aborted after the decree of verse 23, issued by this same Artaxerxes. It was one thing to patronise the religion of a subject people, but quite another to fortify their cities when local people accused them of sedition. Nehemiah, who had perhaps expected better results from Ezra's mission, was deeply wounded (4), and, like Ezra before him, prayed and fasted as a plan formed in his mind. He would himself approach the king for authority to go and put matters right (11). The plan was risky: the powerful like to patronise, not to be persuaded by, their privileged favourites, and he could have been accused of ingratitude.

Nehemiah lacked neither courage nor piety, however. He was more of an activist than Ezra was, and more a leader of men, but he had the same spiritual priorities. He, too, confesses the nation's sin (6,7), honours the power of his God (5), recalls appropriate scriptures (8,9) and history (10), and prays humbly for help in time of need (6,11), not neglecting to express his penitence, and to assist his devotion, by fasting.

In all this there are lessons for us, too. How much do we care about the fate of our fellow-Christians? How willing are we to offer ourselves to do something about it? How willing are we to risk our own prestige and promotion in such an enterprise? How do our prayers match up to the standard of Nehemiah's prayer? His action serves to underline the fact that God is not only served by priests and scholars, but by laymen, too, who are willing to use their position for him. See, for a touching example of courage, Matthew 27:57–61.

THOUGHT: Consider Matthew 27:57–61 as a touching example of a layman using his position and possessions to serve God.

2 Faith overcomes obstacles

Four months later opportunity came (1). That, despite his fear (2), Nehemiah should have spoken out to such effect (3, 5, 7–8) provides an Old Testament illustration of Jesus' promise in Luke 21:14–15, for Nehemiah experienced God's overruling hand (8), doubtless as a result of his urgent prayer before he uttered his request (4). It is a rewarding experience to rely on God's promises and find them true. Nehemiah could so easily have said, and thus achieved, nothing.

Ever the practical man, he arranged for letters from the emperor to ensure local co-operation and supplies (7, 8), and was furnished with an armed escort – no other companions are mentioned. On arrival in the province he encountered his first obstacle, the displeasure of San-ballat and Tobiah. The first is called governor of Samaria in contemporary papyri from Egypt, and was probably not a Jew (see 13:28). His name is Babylonian, but he may have been a worshipper of Yahweh, God of Israel, since, according to the same papyri, his sons bore names compounded with -yah. 'Horonite' indicates that he was a native of the area, from one of three places thus named. Tobiah was also a worshipper of Yahweh, but an Ammonite (compare Gen. 19:38; Deut. 23:3), and probably a senior civil servant of the Persian government in nearby Ammon (across the Jordan). These men were leaders of the local people who, even before the time of Ezra's mission, had opposed the Babylonian Jewish re-settlement of Judah, and they had Arab support from the south (19).

Nehemiah's preference for autocratic methods appears in verses 11–16. Very often the less said about one's intentions, the less opposition will be stirred up. He made a secret, night-time inspection of the south and east walls of the city, examining them from both directions. Obviously they were in considerable disrepair (14). He was now in a position to declare his plans and his announcement yielded immediate results. The Jews were willing to help.

The opposition and derision of the local governors, who once again tried to pin a charge of sedition upon the Jews (see Ezra 4:14–16), led Nehemiah to endorse the earlier judgement of the same community, namely that the new city was not for them, but for the returned exiles, who were true servants of the God of heaven (20; see Ezra 4:3). How this policy developed we shall see later, but it was rooted in the conviction expressed at the beginning of the verse, 'The God of heaven will make us prosper'. It is such faith that moves mountains (Matt. 21:21, 22).

3;4 Hard work

Chapter 3: Rebuilding the wall was an enormous task, requiring careful planning, and Nehemiah must have had considerable organising and negotiating ability. It is encouraging to see so many and such varied groups of people hard at work: town groups from all over Judah (2–5 etc.), the high priest himself (1), whose house was now part of the extended city wall (20, 21), people from outside local jurisdiction (7) whose help may have been quite unexpected, the gangs under the leadership of their local squires – some of these groups more enthusiastic than others (5). Lord, in verse 5, is almost certainly not a reference to God but, if singular, to Nehemiah, and, if plural, to the city rulers including Nehemiah. The wall was divided into forty sections, listed in anticlockwise order. On the north and west of the city, it was rebuilt along the existing line, but on the east where the references are to private houses, a new line was adopted along the ridge of the hill, possibly with a view to incorporating a larger population. Such was the commitment of these volunteers to the enterprise that at least two groups (4, 21 and 5, 27 – the latter despite their nobles!) managed a second section of wall.

Chapter 4: Despite the jealous taunts of Sanballat and Tobiah (1–3) the wall made good progress (6), owing to the people's enthusiasm and Nehemiah's uncompromising leadership. His prayer (4, 5) reflects perhaps more of his personal temperament than would be appropriate for a Christian today (Matt. 5:43–48; 6:14, 15), but his jealousy for God's own feelings is noteworthy (4, 5). Since mere words did not have the desired effect, Israel's enemies, reinforced by Philistines from Ashdod (7), now resorted to violence (8). Verse 9 is a model response for all Christian workers. God has no hands but ours. We should exhibit the serpent's cunning as well as the dove's gentleness (Matt. 10:16). Though the workers were tired (10), when they were warned of threatened attack (12, 13) they took thorough protective measures (13, 16–20). Nehemiah also reminded them of the greatness of their God. So they were physically, mentally and spiritually prepared (14). An encouraging chapter in the New Testament addressed to persecuted and divided Christians is Hebrews 12. There too (1–3) a secret of power is to 'consider Jesus'.

In the event, battle was not joined (15). The work went on, this time closely guarded with vigilance by day and by night. Like a good leader, Nehemiah himself was there in the thick of it (23), not discouraged by the temporary interruption of the work, but seemingly made more determined by it. A problem is either an insuperable obstacle or an exciting challenge. With God it need never be the former (see Mark 9:23; 10:27; Phil. 4:13).

QUESTION: How far does 4:9 reflect your priorities and those of your church?

5 A problem within the community

This hard-working community spoiled its witness by failure in finance. It was apparently a time of scarcity (3), and to buy food the poor had had to sell their children into pledge. This is the most probable meaning of verse 2: RSV 'with' is not present in the text, and 'many' becomes 'mortgaging' by a slight change. For the practice see Exodus 21:2. Others had to mortgage their lands to buy food (3) – at 12 per cent interest, if verse 11 means a hundredth per month – or to pay the imperial tax. The grievances are summarised in verse 5. According to Jewish law, interest could only be exacted from a foreigner (Deut. 23:19, 20), and Hebrew slaves (Deut. 15:12) had to be released after six years' service. It is not clear whether the oppressors were the rich amongst the new settlers (7), taking advantage of the poor, or whether it was the new community treating as foreigners the local Jews who had not been exiled (some had been enslaved, 8), hence the appeal in verse 5 to their common ancestry. The latter is more likely, and more reprehensible, since Nehemiah's entourage had made a point of redeeming and financing them (8, 10). To oppress them again was to betray their declared purposes.

Nehemiah called a meeting of all the people (7) at which he condemned the leaders' actions and demanded immediate restitution. They agreed, but he felt it necessary to summon priests to administer an oath (12, 13). In the ceremony he performed a piece of prophetic symbolism (compare Ezek. 4:1–3), and the people bore witness to God's righteous opposition to this sin (compare Deut. 27:15–26).

Failure of mutual love amongst God's people is a breach of the second great command (Matt. 22:34–40), and is often expressed in financial selfishness (see 1 Tim. 6:10).

Nehemiah was governor of Judah (14), at least equal in rank to Sanballat in Samaria. His household expenses were heavy (17, 18), yet, unlike the previous governors (15), he paid all the expenses himself. He did not draw the payment to which he was entitled (14, compare Paul, 2 Thess. 3:7–9) or take any land (16). The 'fear of God' (15) prevented any other course, and Nehemiah expected the pious Jew's reward from God (19, compare Prov. 11:4, 24, 25).

Concern for the poor and needy is a frequent theme in the prophets and psalms, and lies at the heart of the law (see Lev. 25:35–55). Failure here constitutes contempt for God himself, the Creator and Saviour of all men (see Matt. 7:12). Religion which ignores the needy is not true religion (Jas. 1:27).

Jerusalem in the time of Nehemiah

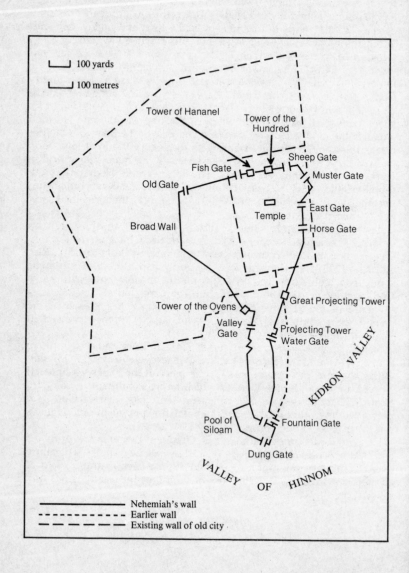

100 yards

100 metres

Tower of Hananel

Tower of the Hundred

Fish Gate

Sheep Gate

Muster Gate

Old Gate

Temple

East Gate

Broad Wall

Horse Gate

Tower of the Ovens

Great Projecting Tower

Valley Gate

Projecting Tower

Water Gate

KIDRON VALLEY

Pool of Siloam

Fountain Gate

Dung Gate

VALLEY OF HINNOM

—————— Nehemiah's wall
- - - - - - - - Earlier wall
– – – – – – – Existing wall of old city

6 How to face slander

Nehemiah was also up against attempts to discredit him personally. First, efforts were made to get him to abandon his work for discussions (1–4), then to discredit his motives (5–9), then to impugn his courage (10–14) and finally to infiltrate his entourage (17–19). Nehemiah's suspicion of the motives of Sanballat and the others was probably justified (2, compare 4:11). The plain of Ono was neutral territory, bordering on Philistia and Samaria, and Nehemiah's enemies were from both districts (4:7). It would have been an ideal place for a kidnapping or a murder. In any case, the time for conferences, as Christian experience in the twentieth century shows, is when the work is *not* being well done, rather than when it is (3).

The second and third assaults upon his integrity were more subtle. The letter of accusation was an open letter (5), for anyone to read and gossip about. The charge was treason, and Artaxerxes had reason to fear a king in Judah (Ezra 4:12–16). To make matters worse, Nehemiah's religious honesty was attacked, for it was said he had bribed prophets to support his treasonable cause (7). Once again his rugged common sense came to the rescue. A flat denial, and no further comment, was all that was required (8). His actions were witness enough to his sense of duty to king and people. But the occasion served as a useful stimulus to renewed prayer (9).

Though the altar could be used for sanctuary (1 Kings 2:28), the Temple was only open to priests. The lay worshippers filled the courts outside. Shemaiah, the hired agent in the third stratagem, may have been a prophet (compare 14). If so, it was Nehemiah's opponents who stooped to bribing prophets. Nehemiah was to be persuaded to enter the Temple for security from a night attack, at the expense of his reputation for piety and courage. Both however were vindicated, for he saw through the ruse, and refused. Fear can make one foolish, but faith brings salvation (Hab. 2:4).

Thus Nehemiah's adversaries were reduced to using the well-connected Tobiah (his family is possibly the one which features prominently in a Transjordanian inscription a couple of centuries later, and which at one stage purchased the high-priesthood) to infiltrate the governor's entourage with spies and smooth-tongued peacemakers. The threatening letters continued. But at least the wall was finished (15), and Nehemiah's perseverance won the day, resulting in serious loss of face for the surrounding peoples (15, 16). Despite all the opposition, it was now clear whose side God was on. For Christian experience of this see Romans 8:31–39.

7;8 The place of the law

A great deal had by now been achieved (1), and Jerusalem was ready for its own governor. Nehemiah chose well: his brother Hanani had been the original inspiration of the work, and Hananiah was both experienced and godly (2). The newly-walled city needed guarding, especially as its population was still quite small (3, 4). In building the wall first, despite the attendant discomforts, Nehemiah had his priorities right.

A register of the population became desirable to facilitate government (5), and a list of the original returned exiles was used as a basis (6–73a, compare Ezra 2). Nehemiah's own register has not survived, and we cannot know whether the entitlement problems of verses 61–65 were ever resolved. Urim and Thummim were probably stones used by the high priests for drawing lots when making choices (see Exod. 28:30).

The (still largely rural) community could now, however, be gathered, according to the law (Lev. 23:24) to re-dedicate itself to obedience to the law of Moses (73b; 8:1). This act of allegiance was more comprehensive than that of Ezra 10, which only concerned mixed marriages. It was probably only possible because of the strong political identity which Nehemiah had given the people. If a strict sequence is followed this event began only a week after the completion of the wall (6:15). Here the editor of our books interpolates part of the story of Ezra and Nehemiah's memoir is resumed in 11:1. Ezra was obviously the man to preside, both in virtue of his royal mandate (Ezra 7:12–26) and of his own personal skills (Ezra 7:6). The law was perhaps read in Hebrew (see v. 3), and maybe then translated into the everyday Aramaic (7, 8), unless RSV's 'clearly' (8) be rendered 'with an interpretation', in which case a few words of commentary may have been added. But probably time would preclude this (3). Verses 9–18 describe the holiday which was holy to the Lord (9–11). Though the people might have feared God's judgement, they were to rejoice in his mercy, and this joy would restore their flagging morale (10). It is a great thing when people understand, not just hear, God's word (12, compare Matt. 28:19, 20; Mark 4:34; Luke 24:45–49; John 16:29; 1 Cor. 14:19, 24, 25). Then the first Feast of Tabernacles to be observed properly since Joshua's day was held (17), as the law prescribed for this season (Deut. 16:13–15). The mixture of reading from the law, liturgical celebration, and great rejoicing is a pattern for the Christian community today. The living in temporary shelters was not only a reminder of the Exodus wanderings, but symbolic of the people's building priorities in the city (7:4), and is for us a useful picture of the temporary nature of our present existence (Heb. 13:14).

9 A covenant is made

A fast was then held (1), for the purpose of further law-reading and worship – this time confession (3). The mood had changed, and Israel alone (2) stood before its God in penitence for past sin, in intercession for present distress (36, 37), and to make a covenant (38) before God, i.e. an undertaking to obey him. Their spokesman was probably Ezra again (as in the Greek text of verse 6), and his prayer is in a tradition characteristic of Jewish piety, recalling past events to illustrate the character both of God and of Israel – compare Psalms 78, 105, 106, Ezra 9:6–15; Daniel 9:4–19, etc. The lessons of history are still there for the Christian worshipper to ponder. It is not clear why taxation was suddenly reintroduced as a cause of distress in this otherwise joyful occasion (36, 37), but it remains true that no celebration this side of heaven can be untinged with grief at this world's injustices (Eccl. 7:2; Matt. 5:4).

Notice the things that seemed important to Ezra. He recalled the great power of God (11) and the ingratitude of Israel (16). God's generosity and mercy (13–15, 17, 19), his guidance, provision and gift of land (20–25) are contrasted with Israel's disobedience (26). The lessons were repeated (26–31), but unlearned. Therefore (32–38), in their present distress the people could still appeal to God's kindness and reaffirm their commitment to the gracious covenant God had given them (compare Exod. 24:8). Maybe this time they had learned. It is with relief that Christians can recall that forgiveness is now sealed in Christ's blood, and there need be no uncertainty about it any more (1 John 1:6–9; Rom. 5:1; 8:1). Hebrews 9 repays study in this connection.

FOR PRAISE AND WORSHIP. ' . . .how much more shall the blood of Christ, who through the eternal Spirit offered himself without blemish to God, purify your conscience from dead works to serve the living God' (Hebrews 9:14).

10;11 The law is accepted

The covenant binding Israel to obey God was sealed (9:38) and a list ensues of the 'signatories' (10:1–27). The seals would be in clay. That the old covenant was written on tablets, but the new on our hearts was anticipated by Jeremiah (31:31–34) and recognised by Paul (2 Cor. 3:3), who applies it to the testimony of his converts' lives, as well as to the gospel message (2 Cor. 3:6). The language of this undertaking (28–39) is Deuteronomic: it refers again to mixed marriages (30, Deut. 7:3), to careful obedience to the laws (29, Deut. 26:16), to sabbath observance (31, Deut. 5:12–15), and offering first-fruits to God (35–37) as tithes (see Deut. 12:6; 14:23–25; 26:1–10). But other parts of the law are alluded to. With verse 32 compare 2 Chronicles 24:6 and Exodus 13:11–16; with verse 33, Exodus 40:23, and see also Numbers 28:1–8. Only the wood offering (34) is unknown in the law of Moses as we have it now (compare Lev. 6:12, 13). Sabbath observance was especially important to Nehemiah (the first signatory, 1), as the events of 13:15–22 make clear. It was now becoming a mark of the observant Jew, and was seen as a blessing rather than a burden (Isa. 58:13, 14). The joy of the law is very evident here, and an indication of Ezra's ministry is found in the final sentence of the chapter. By such obedience there was hope of new life (see Lev. 18:5, a favourite text of Paul, Rom. 10:5; Gal. 3:12).

Chapter 11 resumes Nehemiah's memoir, left off at 7:4, 5, the old census list and Ezra's law-reading having intervened. The need for a reasonable population for the newly-walled city (7:4) was solved by drawing lots. The sense of privilege involved is indicated by the use of 'holy city' to describe Jerusalem (that this would be a phrase used by the restored community is already predicted in Isaiah 48:2, compare 52:1), and by the blessing they were given (2). To move there, so soon after their arrival in the land, would be a second great upheaval for the families concerned, but they willingly accepted the verdict of the lot. Once again all classes of society were included (3–19) and there was also a representative of the Emperor (24). The list in verses 3–19 is basically that of 1 Chronicles 9:2–18. There are some differences because of the work of the Chronicler. The rural population had expanded, too, into a number of border towns (20–36). For an anticipation of this growth in population, especially in Jerusalem, see Isaiah 54:1–3.

THOUGHT: 'Sabbath observance . . .was seen as a blessing rather than a burden'. Relate this to your feelings about the Christian Sunday.

12 The wall is dedicated

The lists of chapter 11 are followed, for the sake of completeness, by a list of the chief amongst the priests (1–7) and of the Levites (8, 9) who were contemporaries of the first post-exilic high priest, Joshua (compare Ezra 2:2; 3:2) – supplementing Ezra 2:36–42. Next comes a list of the hereditary high priests down to the time of the invasion of Alexander of Macedon (10, 11; Jaddua held that office, according to Josephus, in 333 BC when the invaders arrived). These last two verses may have been brought up to date by later scribes after the publication of Ezra-Nehemiah, which was probably in the first quarter of the fourth century BC. It was important from a legal and ceremonial point of view to establish 'who's who' in Judah (entitlement to land and certain priestly, ceremonial and other functions depended on proof of descent). Also later generations would depend on these lists for vital information, for example, about marriage contracts, which might breach the Mosaic injunctions against marriage with foreigners (compare also 13:1–3). Priests of the next generation are then recorded (12–21) and Levites (22–26) up to the time of Darius III ('the Persian' 22, so-called to distinguish him from Darius I, or possibly from 'Darius the Mede', who is unknown outside the book of Daniel, e.g. Dan. 5:31; 6:28). The Johanan of verse 22 is the Jonathan of verse 11, anachronistically referred to in Ezra 10:6, probably written when he actually was high priest. The mention of Nehemiah in the third person in verses 26 and 47 reinforces the impression that he made use of an official archive when he compiled his memoirs. Godly men, above all others, should be painstaking and accurate in their work.

In verse 27 the story is resumed to record the dedication of the wall. It had been built for God, and with his protection. Now that it was completed, God was not to be forgotten. It is a proper thing for Christians, too, to offer such formal acknowledgement of the power of God which underlies even the most secular work when it has been done for him. Two great ritual processions went around the walls and surrounded the city from opposite directions. Ezra led one group (36) and Nehemiah went with the other group (38). Once again the city's rejoicing could be heard at a distance, for it was a family occasion too (43). Officers were then appointed to administer the Temple stores (44–47), by now a substantial task. The picture conveyed by this account is of strength, unity, security, and joy, and the secret is in verse 43. God had given them their joy, as well as the immediate causes of it. He is still the same (Phil. 4:4; John 15:11, compare Neh. 8:10).

FOR MEDITATION: 'Without having seen him you love him; though you do not now see him you believe in him and rejoice with unutterable and exalted joy' (1 Peter 1:8).

13 More problems

Good beginnings are no guarantee of happy endings. The people ought to have been aware of the law's requirements about the racial purity of Israel (Deut. 23:3–6), but only now did they act on them (1–3). Furthermore, during Nehemiah's absence on a visit to the king (6) Tobiah the Ammonite (see 2:19; 6:17–19) had so ingratiated himself with Eliashib (perhaps the later high priest, 28) that he had lodgings provided for him in the Temple courts themselves, despite the events of verse 3. Upon Nehemiah's return he had to be evicted (4–9). Nehemiah had left in 433 BC to return to court, but still had the Emperor's confidence in his governorship, and was not required to remain in Susa, the capital. (The title 'king of Babylon' in verse 6 appears to be a Jewish designation for all Nebuchadnezzar's successors, even the Persian emperors.) Then it was found that the tithes had not been paid, so an economic commission of four (a priest, a scribe, a Levite and a layman) was appointed to deal with this. Nehemiah, like Ezra (see Ezra 8:33), was learning to delegate.

Sabbath observance was another practice to be honoured more in the breach than in the observance (15–22), the profit motive being then, as nowadays, uppermost. The truth of Isaiah 58:13, 14 had not been learned, and the covenant was once more broken (see 9:38). And then mixed marriages began to creep back, despite the earlier vows (Ezra 10:5; Neh. 10:30, 31), the lesson of Solomon himself (1 Kings 11:4) and the law in which the people professed to rejoice (Deut. 7:3, 4). Even one of Johanan's brothers (28) was amongst the offenders, and matters can hardly have been helped by his disloyal choice of father-in-law. For the source of Nehemiah's distress in verse 29 see Leviticus 21:14, where the Greek text goes further than the Hebrew in restricting a priest's choice of wife to Levites.

What more could Nehemiah have done? It is required of God's servants that they be faithful, not necessarily successful (1 Cor. 4:1–5), and this Nehemiah certainly was (14, 22, 31). Ezra's liturgical expertise and biblical scholarship, together with Nehemiah's firm leadership and political skill, combined in each man with genuine reverence for God, had set the Jewish people on a new course. The future was full of promise if they would keep the covenant they had made. But, as history relates, only one man, by his obedience, was ever able to undo the work of faithless generations (Rom. 5:18, 19).

THOUGHT: It is required of God's servants that they be found faithful, not necessarily successful.

Questions for further study and discussion on Nehemiah

1. What can be learnt from the recorded prayers of Nehemiah?

2. *I am only one, but I am one.*
I can't do everything, but I can do something.
What I can do, I ought to do.
What I ought to do,
By the grace of God, I will do.
When Nehemiah heard about the plight of Jerusalem what successive steps did he take? What do you find challenging and helpful about this?

3. We are surrounded by calls upon our sympathy and service. How can we decide what God wants us to do?

4. Look again at Nehemiah's use of his home and resources. In what ways does having a home and family affect one's commitment to serve others?

5. 'It is a rewarding experience to rely on God's promises and find them true' (see notes on Neh. 2). Discuss times in your life when you have experienced this. Why do we so often fail to experience it?

6. Are there lessons for us in the ways in which opposition is countered in this book?

7. 'Failure of mutual love amongst God's people is often expressed in financial selfishness' (see notes on Nehemiah 5). How does the attitude of Nehemiah differ from that of the leaders of the people? Discuss how we can recognise financial selfishness in our lives, and rid ourselves of it.

8. Is there any value, do you think, in the expression of spiritual truths and commitments in liturgical form, as is frequently done in Ezra and Nehemiah?

9. What is the place in the life of the Christian of the keeping of laws such as tithing and sabbath observance (Nehemiah 13, compare Rom. 14; Rev. 2:18–29)?

Introduction

ESTHER.

In this book we are far from the carefully recorded personal and official memoirs of Ezra and Nehemiah, and instead in the world of the popular story writer. The story explains the reason for observing the Festival of Purim (9:26–28), first referred to in 2 Maccabees 15:36, in which Jewish revenge on Gentile anti-semitism is celebrated. It reflects some of the interests of second and first-century Jews, and its composition in writing may date from around then. Its Jewish hero and heroine are not mentioned in the list of famous men in Ecclesiasticus 44–50, and indeed the book itself does not feature in some early Christian canons of scripture, nor in at least one Jewish canon. Only 10:2 refers to a source (otherwise unknown) for the story, and the complete absence of a mention of God (though see 4:14) has been a contributory factor in many Christians' strong disapproval of the book (Luther wished it had never been written!). It is, however, a valuable example of the literature of Diaspora Judaism, and a gripping and well-told story, although by New Testament standards its theological ideas are rather limited.

1 A disastrous party

Verses 1–9 tell of an extravagant party held by Xerxes I (Ahasuerus, 485–465) in 483, some twenty-five years before the mission of Ezra. Every detail in the account is intended to exaggerate the Emperor's wealth, power and generosity. The queen's refusal to comply with his idiotic and vain demand does her credit (10–12). Herodotus calls her Amestris. The name Vashti is otherwise unknown as Xerxes' queen. Verses 13–22 record Ahasuerus' wounded self-love expressing itself in a petty revenge with the support of sycophantic magi (13). The decree in verse 22 is pointless, merely reinforcing the existing obligation on any head of a household to make sure his orders are understood.

The villains of this chapter are not the Emperor and his court alone, but the very human vices of conceit, over-indulgence in drink, and lack of trust and respect between the sexes. The New Testament shows that all three can be dealt with by Christ (Rom. 12:1–3; Eph. 5:17–20; 1 Pet. 3:1–7), though they can still mar the church's witness in the modern world.

2 God's plan is formed

A few years have elapsed (2:16, compare 1:3: this is 479 BC), and the imperial harem was to be restocked with girls, from whose number a new queen might be selected. Concubinage is nowhere prohibited in the Bible, though Christian deacons are, according to one interpretation of 1 Timothy 3:12, advised to have only one wife. Monogamy has usually been the rule amongst Christians.

The relevance of this story to God's people now emerges. Mordecai is said to have been a Jew in the capital, Susa, who had once lived in Jerusalem before being exiled in 597 BC, in the reign of Jehoiachin (here called Jeconiah as in Jer. 24:1, and also Coniah in Jer. 22:24). This means he would have been at least 116 years old by this time and if Esther was his cousin (7), even if a generation younger than he, she would doubtless be a little elderly for this kind of adventure. An alternative possibility is that Kish (5) was the contemporary of Jeconiah. Mordecai's name is Babylonian, and it is more reasonable to assume he was born amongst the exiled Jews in Babylon, and prudently moved to Susa in the Persian period to be near the court, and thus the centre of power. It seems Mordecai had some access to court circles (see 11, 22). Hadassah means Myrtle, and is a Jewish name. Esther is either Babylonian (like Mordecai, the name of a deity), or Persian, meaning a star. There is nothing unusual about having two names. Esther, in the good providence of God (though the story does not expressly say so) found herself not only in the harem (8), but quickly recognised as one of its most attractive members (9). She was not only beautiful, but loyal (10, 20) and obedient (15). Whether it was prudence or fear that prevented her revealing her race is unclear (10). For that year (12) she could not have lived as a practising Jew, but that is not the point of the story. Her promotion to queen was rapid (15–18), and further prepared the way for God to use her for his people. *Tebeth* (16) is an alternative name for the month unknown elsewhere in the Bible.

But it was Mordecai to whom the chance next came to find favour at court (19–23). His attendance around court circles paid off, and his concern for the Emperor's well-being was, in the best Persian bureaucratic tradition, recorded. Each event occurred at the right moment in God's time, and reminds us of such statements as Romans 8:28, and as Galatians 4:4. But waiting is often hard (Jas. 5:7–11; Luke 21:19; Hab. 2:3), and the niceties of religious observance do not always seem as important as they ought (compare Acts 15:29 with 1 Cor. 8:4–8). Contrast, though, Daniel 1:8–16.

3 The enemy of the Jews

No reason need be given by an autocrat for the promotion of a favourite, and Haman seems to have had no qualities that would justify his elevation to the high office of Grand Vizier. By calling him an Agagite (1), our author is perhaps suggesting he was of the family of Agag, King of the Amalekites, the ancient enemies of the Jews (see 1 Sam. 15:32, 33; Exod. 17:14–16). For Mordecai to make the required obeisance would thus not only have been potentially blasphemous, but also disloyal to the Jewish race, membership of which he now freely confessed (4). It sometimes takes a crisis to bring out one's real convictions (see John 19:38; 7:50–52). Haman's unbalanced reaction has modern parallels, and Christians should not think they are exempt from such persecution. Racial hatred in any form is a sin (Col. 3:11; Acts 17:26, 27).

Like many an insane megalomaniac, Haman was superstitious (7). His belief that some days are, in the eternal order of things, more propitious for certain courses of action than others, is shared by millions today. They are wrong, for God is bound neither by the accidents of chance nor by the movements of the stars (Isa. 44:24, 25; 47:12–15). Haman's 10,000 silver talents were a bribe – the Emperor was not going to have to finance the evil and expensive operation. Had he had any sense of duty he would have stopped it – see Romans 13:1–7 for the task of rulers.

It had taken a year to find an auspicious date for the pogrom, and a year was to elapse before its execution, in 473 BC (7, 12, 13). The plans, were made thoroughly (12–14), as is often the case when evil men are diabolically inspired, but Haman had failed to reckon with God. Much was to happen before the story's end, and God's instruments, Esther and Mordecai, were already prepared and in place. Furthermore, popular opinion had been left out of account (15), and no amount of merry drinking would render the government safe from the views of the people. Everyone knew that the slanderous accusations of verse 8 were merely window-dressing – there was nothing to back them up. Christians, too, must be prepared for such misrepresentations (1 Pet. 4:12–19).

QUESTION: How does racial hatred show itself in your community? What more could your church fellowship do to combat it?

4;5 The plot thickens

Chapter 4: It was amongst the Jewish people, naturally, that the horror was most keenly felt, and their reaction was to go into premature mourning (1,3). But Mordecai knew where he might find help (2). Panic had not numbed his intelligence. For advice to Christians experiencing persecution and difficulties see Hebrews 10:32–39.

In the seclusion of the harem the queen had heard nothing of all this, and had to be told (4–9). She knew she might risk her life by intervening (10,11), the custom here referred to is known by Herodotus, but Mordecai had to remind her that if she did not her fate was sealed in any case (13,14). The argument was crude, and Esther's choice agonising. The inspiration to obey Mordecai yet again (see 2:20) came from her fear of God (14), and recognition of his hand in her promotion. It takes courage to use high office in the cause of justice, but there is no excuse for cowardice. Spiritual resources such as those used in verses 15–17 may have been the reason for Esther's ultimate success, and feature largely in books about this period (see Ezra 8:21; Neh. 1:4–11; Dan. 10:2–3). Christians, too, should use them (Matt. 6:16–18). It was now Mordecai's turn to be obedient (17), and he did not demur.

Chapter 5: In the event Esther moved slowly. She might have spoken at once when she knew she would be well received (3), but either her nerve failed her, or she wished to confront Haman in person. Either way, her plan appealed to the king, whose enjoyment of a party has already been highlighted (ch. 1), and was bound to go down well. In the same way Jesus knew what Levi would enjoy (Matt. 9:9, 10; compare Luke 16:1–9). The King's repeated promise (3, 6) was doubtless merely conventional (see Mark 6:23), but encouraging also. According to the Greek text of verse 8 the dinner party lasted two days. The Hebrew text suggests, probably incorrectly (see 12), that the King's invitation occurred during drinks before dinner.

In this story all the characters act true to form, and yet God is behind it all (see 4:14). Thus Haman preened himself, and boasted of his success with the royal couple, but was in consequence even more riled by Mordecai's discourtesy (9–13). The plan devised by his wife and cronies to execute Mordecai before the next day's party rather discredits the superstitious care recorded in 3:7, and the haughty disdain of 3:6, but also creates further suspense, for must not the queen's plan now fail? At such times it is clear that salvation comes from God alone (Psalm 94).

6;7 God's timing

One of the most memorable features of this book is the timing of the events it records, and these two chapters illustrate this magnificently. At the same time as Haman was seeking Mordecai's death, the king was deciding to honour him (6:1,2). The very ambition Haman outlined for himself was bestowed upon his enemy, the Jew (6:3–11). At precisely the point where the king found himself unable to revoke or punish Haman's cruelty, Haman himself provided an excuse (7:8). And on the very gallows which he had just built for Mordecai, Haman was hanged (7:9,10). No reader of Esther need be in doubt that behind all the events staged upon our world there lies the sovereign hand of God to permit or to restrain, to initiate or to conclude the actions of his creature, man.

The book of memorabilia (1) would be intended to remind the king of his own greatness. That the passage chosen that night concerned Mordecai was yet another of God's coincidences (2), compare 2:21–23. But the real sign that God's purposes were not to be overthrown came when Haman had to lead Mordecai on the crowned horse through Susa (9, 11), proclaiming his royal favour. As Haman's magi well knew (13), it was an inauspicious episode with which to begin the evil plot. So sharply had his mood changed that Haman seems to have been unprepared for the queen's banquet (14), which was to be the scene of his downfall.

As before (5:6), it was after dinner, and under the influence of wine, that the king, by now aware that a great matter was afoot, enquired about Esther's petition (7:2). Her moment had come, and she rose to it (3–6). Clearly Xerxes was unaware that Haman's plan (3:8,9) was directed against the Jews, a people whom the Persians usually treated with some respect. It is not clear whether Haman or the king knew that Esther herself was Jewish. Nonetheless, angry though the king was, he was powerless to rescind a decree sealed with his own ring (compare Dan. 6:14,15, in which story, too, the Emperor, for a different reason, found that sleep eluded him as God acted to save his servant). But Haman in his abject fear provided a convenient excuse for his own arrest (8), and with covered face (Persian emperors were shielded from all distressing sights at court) he was led away to face the cruel fate he had planned for Mordecai. Only then was the king placated (10).

To remind ourselves of how man proposes and God disposes, it is illuminating to read Proverbs 16:1–18, which this story well illustrates.

8 Light for God's people

There still remained a nine-month interval before the pogrom organised by Haman and his friends was due to take place (9, see 3:13), but the whole far-flung empire needed to be apprised of any change of plan. Haman having been executed as a traitor, his house was forfeit (compare Ezra 6:11, NEB), and the Emperor chose to give it to his Jewish Queen. She, knowing to whom she owed her deliverance, set Mordecai over Haman's household – a nice piece of divine irony. Mordecai, moreover, received Haman's office as vizier (2) – a popular choice (15).

It then became necessary to counteract the effects of the previous royal decree (3:12–15), which could not itself be countermanded. Such irresponsible delegation of authority to favourites can do untold harm. Hence, at the queen's further request (3–6), letters were written to the Jewish communities of the empire (8), under royal seal and by the royal secretariat (9), and with great urgency (10, for Haman's arrangements would already have been begun throughout the empire), with copies to the local governors. These allowed the Jews to arm and defend themselves, and to take booty from any enemies who might attack them (11–14). The bureaucratic chaos is laughable, but the brutality of the events that ensued is tragic. Even if violence may be used in self-defence, it is sad if bad government makes it necessary (see Matt. 18:7, NIV).

A good consequence of all this was that the Jews won a great deal of popular sympathy and support – after all, in those unpredictable days it might next be the turn of any other race – even to the extent of gaining some proselytes (15–17). It is the way of God to turn dark deeds to good, and to bring out of sorrow new light and joy. The conviction of the Psalmist (Ps. 30:5) remains the experience of many today, and finds its richest illustration in the events of Good Friday and Easter Day (Rom. 4:25).

THOUGHT: ' . . . you will weep and lament, but the world will rejoice; you will be sorrowful, but your sorrow will turn into joy' (John 16:20).

9;10 Celebrating great events

The popular sympathy and support the Jews enjoyed must have been considerably reduced after the events of chapter 9. In the face of such widespread slaughter boasting should be moderated by grief rather than enhanced by festivities. Presumably there were those still committed to fulfilling Haman's plan, who lacked the sense to disarm themselves before the influence of an increasingly mighty Jewish vizier (4). The brutality suggested by verse 5 has an all too modern ring. Steps were also taken to prevent any perpetuation of Haman's line (7–10). That the Jews' vengeance was not mixed with greed is, however, clear from verses 10, 15 and 16 (compare 8:11).

It was evidently the custom for the festival of Purim to be kept on two different days, the 14th Adar (about early March) in villages, and the 15th in walled towns (so some Greek manuscripts record explicitly in verse 19). Verses 11–19 are designed to explain this, though why Esther demanded a second day of slaughter in Susa is not explained, except that she also wished to exhibit the bodies of Haman's sons. Mordecai thus decreed that Purim should be observed on both days, and marked by rejoicing, rest and the exchange of gifts. A record of the events which led to the festival's inauguration was compiled (23–32), and this book is still read by Jews today, according to the prescription of verse 28, at the festival season. The picture evoked by the description in verse 22 is delightful, and a model for God's people everywhere. A great event deserves great celebration, and Christians who 'esteem one day as better than another' (Rom. 14:5, 6) stand in a great Old Testament tradition. See also 1 Corinthians 5:7, 8 for a Christian adaptation of an Old Testament festival theme.

Of Mordecai's reputed fame (10:2, 3), and the chronicle mentioned in verse 2, we know nothing from secular sources, and perhaps should not expect to. The exaggerated style of our author makes it unnecessary to seek external confirmation of all his details. Enough to record that God was very gracious to his people at a time of great danger. He raised up two strategically placed people to avert it, and gave them great honour and success in the world of their day. From all this there came a joyful celebration to be observed yearly.

THOUGHT: If these domestic affairs in far-off ancient Persia are still worthy of study and remembrance, how much more those events by which God in his infinite wisdom and love achieved the salvation of the whole world?

Questions for further study and discussion on Esther

1. Should we expect God to deliver his people on every occasion they are threatened? How can we know what to pray for in such situations?

2. How desirable is it for Christians to aspire to high political office, locally or nationally? What are the dangers?

3. Consider the causes and results of Haman's vanity. How can we resist this vice?

4. 'Each event occurred at the right moment in God's time. . . but waiting is often hard.' Discuss your experience of this. What does waiting involve? How can we recognise when God's time has come for us to act?

5. What is the Christian response to acts of aggression?

6. Can a case be made out for moral and religious compromise with secular standards in situations where Christianity is either prohibited or severely controlled?

7. In what ways did the private lives of the people in this book affect their public judgements? Discuss some examples of how the private lives of our national leaders can affect public affairs. Should they therefore be subject to popular scrutiny and restraint?

8. Pray together for the secular and religious leaders of your community, country and of other countries.

Introduction

'The patience of Job' has become proverbial (see Jas. 5:11), but the book that bears his name has even more to offer us than a pattern of how to endure sickness, misunderstanding and bereavement. It is about what God is like, and takes the form of a disputation in which Job, Job's friends and even Satan participate, but in which God has the last word. His wisdom and might are so much greater than Job had ever thought, that both the theological debate and the terrible sufferings of Job are completely dwarfed. As the flurry of words gives place to awed silence and humble trust, God is able to restore the fortunes of his servant, whose sufferings have been the occasion of a new revelation of the nature of God. The book in its present form probably belongs to the sixth century BC, and shares with other exilic literature the task of vindicating the character of Israel's God to her suffering and dispersed people.

Analysis of Job

1:1–2:13 Prologue: Job's integrity and trials
3:1–42:6 Dialogue

3:1–26	Job's lament	
4:1–14:22	First cycle of speeches	
	4:1–5:27	Eliphaz
	6:1–7:21	Job
	8:1–22	Bildad
	9:1–10:22	Job
	11:1–20	Zophar
	12:1–14:22	Job
15:1–21:34	Second cycle of speeches	
	15:1–35	Eliphaz
	16:1–17:16	Job
	18:1–21	Bildad
	19:1–29	Job
	20:1–29	Zophar
	21:1–34	Job
22:1–31:40	Third cycle of speeches	
	22:1–30	Eliphaz
	23:1–24:25	Job
	25:1–6	Bildad
	26:1–31:40	Job
32:1–37:24	The Elihu speeches	
38:1–42:6	The Yahweh speeches	
	38:1–40:2	Yahweh
	40:3–5	Job
	40:6–41:34	Yahweh
	42:1–6	Job

42:7–17 Epilogue: Job's vindication and restoration

1 Disaster strikes

The story begins in North Arabia, where Job is presented as a wealthy landowner with extensive urban and agricultural property (see also 29:7–10). His piety is stated from the start (1), and illustrated by the sacrifices he offered on behalf of his sons (5, where the Greek version specifies sin-offerings, for which see Lev. 4). He has also that other reward of the wealthy righteous in the Old Testament, fame (3b; compare Ezek. 14:14, 20).

As with Goethe's Faust, before the story unfolds we are treated to a prologue in heaven. It seems Job knew nothing of this, and after chapter 2 no further reference is made to it. Other divine council meetings are described or alluded to in 1 Kings 22:19–23; Psalm 82; Isaiah 6; 40:1–9 and Jeremiah 23:18. We do well to recall that according to the Bible, the real issues are being fought out on a higher plane than ours and by greater powers (1 Cor. 2:6–8; Eph. 6:12; Col. 2:15;). Satan is successively pictured as tempter (1 Chron. 21:1), accuser (Zech. 3:1) and fierce opponent of the godly (1 Pet. 5:8, 9), and is said to have great beauty and power (Jude 8, 9). His aim here is to demonstrate that God is only loved by those he prospers (9–11).

Whether Satan is right will in Job's case soon become plain, for Job suffers the loss of all his family and possessions on one calamitous day (13–19). He is not to know it is by divine permission (12) yet his reaction is exemplary (20, 21). For God as the author of calamity see Amos 3:6 and Isaiah 45:7. We need never doubt that God is in ultimate control of our temptations (see 1 Cor. 10:13). It is God's prerogative to give, and his to take away. That he should do either foolishly is unthinkable, for he alone is truly wise. Compare the famous words of Jesus in Gethsemane (Matt. 26:39).

CONSIDER your own reasons for loving God.

2;3 'Not single spies, but in battalions'

The words quoted at the head of these notes are Shakespeare's description of how our troubles come to us. Jesus himself is described in prophecy as 'a man of sorrows' (Isa. 53:3), and the haunting complaint of the devasted city of Jerusalem in Lamentations 1:12 is a memorable expression of the agony experienced by many of God's people in every age. Job chapters 1 and 2 must rank as one of literature's most comprehensive descriptions of human distress. Not only Job's family and property, but even his body, are now all destroyed, for if the cynicism of Satan is to be rebuked Job must suffer physical agony on top of his emotional distress. His wife's advice (9) is foolish: to see death as a friend was a perversion of Jewish teaching (see also 1 Cor. 15:26), and to blaspheme God's name was unjust (see 1:21). It is often hardest to withstand the temptations that come to us through those we love best (see Matt. 16:22, 23), and Job did well to resist (10). The compassion of his friends is expressed less thoughtlessly than that of his wife (13), but becomes in due course hardly more helpful.

Meanwhile, in chapter 3, Job gives expression to all his aching grief in poetry of great poignancy and deep pathos. For a not dissimilar lament see Jeremiah 20:7–18. It is idle for anyone who has not experienced such misery to presume to comment upon these terrible words. Even pagan magicians, with their reputed powers to malign days and seasons, and to arouse the sea-monster which God had quelled at the creation (8, see Ps. 74:12–17), are exhorted to do their utmost to curse Job's birthday. Death, and its presumed peace (11–19), is now rashly preferred by a heart sick with dread (25).

TO THINK OVER: What are the ingredients of true compassion?

4 A possible reason

The poetic style is now continued, except for a brief interruption, until 42:6. Its exalted tone is a suitable vehicle for such weighty discussion. Eliphaz from Teman is another North Arabian, perhaps one of the famed Edomite masters of wisdom (Jer. 49:7). His arguments are simple and few. He knows Job is a good man (1–6), but suffering is a novelty (5). No wonder it hurts. Furthermore, the innocent do not suffer (7–11). His theology is that of Deuteronomy 28, which has some relevance to Job's circumstances. Though he is too polite to say so, Eliphaz thinks Job must be guilty of sin. Finally, this opinion is reinforced by reference to a vision Eliphaz had seen one night (12–21). In a beautifully told narrative, we hear how Eliphaz learnt that man is ephemeral, not eternal (20, 21), imperfect and not faultless (17–19). With this experience seared upon his memory, he cannot conceive that it does not cover Job's case. Like many religious people, he thinks his own experience and wisdom in theological matters need no broadening. In verse 6 he assumes Job will share the same standpoint, though as it transpires Job allows God to lead him on from that point. Let us remember the perils of desiring to teach others about God.

TO THINK OVER: 'Let not many of you become teachers, my brethren, for you know that we who teach shall be judged with greater strictness' (Jas. 3:1).

5 A possible solution

Eliphaz continues his homily. A harsh reminder of Job's spiritual isolation – he can expect no angelic succour (1), for God is the author of his afflictions – leads into a brief meditation on the insecurity of man's life in this world, especially the life of the fool (2–7). There is hope only in God (8–16), and we find here a noble description of some of the characteristics of the God of the Bible. In these poetic chapters the personal name of God, Yahweh, occurs only once, otherwise the more general term, God, is used, for the matters here discussed are not for Israel only, but for all who believe in God. He it is who is Lord of nature (10), as well as of the affairs of man (11–16). He is great (9) and compassionate (11, 15, 16; see Luke 1:48, 49, 51–53), and opposes the proud (see 1 Pet. 5:5; Prov. 3:34).

In consequence, Eliphaz feels he can confidently recommend this God to Job (17–27), and does so eloquently, enumerating many blessings which Job may receive if he 'commits his cause' (8) to God. The blessings are tempting: restoration from sickness, deliverance from trouble (see Ps. 91:5–8), from famine, from war, and from slander. He will enjoy harmony with his environment, safety, many descendants and long life. What Eliphaz, in all his earnest and well-meaning kindness, has quite forgotten is that Job had indeed trusted God, and found that this experience was not always true. For a while he had known such blessings, but they had been taken away. Christians, too, must be careful not to make promises to people in God's name which are only partly in accord with what we know of God's character. Job is, in fact, more to be commended than Eliphaz, for his faith is unimpaired despite the absence of such prosperity. He had not trusted God merely because of the blessings he had received, as Satan had suggested (1:9–11).

TO THINK OVER: Does Eliphaz' rather thoughtless and superficial listing of the blessings of following God say anything about our evangelistic methods?

6 God and man both blamed

A cycle of speeches now becomes apparent. As each friend concludes his turn, Job offers a response. This is Job's first response to Eliphaz, and he has much to say. It is in reality addressed more to God, for Eliphaz has made points which, though true, are largely irrelevant. But on one issue Job offers a challenge: he is hurt by the suggestion that he is being punished, and calls Eliphaz unkind (14–23). He might have expected encouragement, but has received only rebukes. The loyalty of such friends is like the waters of a wadi, gone in summer, or like the caravans between Tema and Sheba which, though eagerly expected, never arrive (15–20). Job had asked for nothing that would have cost them anything (22, 23). He didn't even get their moral support. For them theology has taken the place of compassion (24–27), as Jesus said it had for the Pharisees of his day (Matt. 23:23, 24; Luke 11:46). It is all too easy for this still to happen in the lives of modern Christians for whom maintaining the integrity of systematic theologies is more important than actually living as the bearers of God's love in his world.

But Job has a complaint against God as well. God's might is arrayed against him (4), and his arrows are poisoned (compare Ps. 38:2). In the rhetorical style of the wisdom writers, used, too, with great effect by Amos (3:3–8), Job asserts that his very wordiness is evidence of the starvation he is experiencing through lack of appreciation by God of the weight of his distress (1–7). The alternative is to die (8–10), for he knows he is innocent (10b), and there is nothing left worth living for (11): his own resources are all spent (12, 13). Once again it is worth pointing out the similarity of Jesus' experience: deserted by his friends (Matt. 26:56), he felt deserted by God also, at his moment of greatest need (Matt. 27:46). But for him too there had been a prologue in heaven, and there was to be a glorious outcome.

QUESTION: Is there 'nothing worth living for'?

7 The silence of God

The silence of God is almost deafening in these chapters, in marked contrast with the verbosity of the speakers. Ecclesiastes 5:2 is a good example of the opinions of the Old Testament wisdom writers on talking (compare Job 38:2). But at this point Job continues with his tirade, and is now full of self-pity. Neither day nor night bring pleasure (1–6), and his days are numbered (7–10) with death as their bitter conclusion. So he feels entitled to cry out against God's treatment of him (11–21). All he wants now is to be left alone by God (16), and he savagely satirises (17) the pious confidence of the Psalmist (see Ps. 8:3–8) that God's concern with man is entirely beneficial (as does Amos, compare Amos 9:2–4; Ps. 139:7–12). In bold contrast to the presupposition of the Psalms, and the priestly blessing (Num. 6:24–26), Job demands that God avert his gaze (19), whose purpose he sees as mere curiosity about how Job will cope. He almost admits to being a sinner (21), and demands forgiveness if it is needed. When he looks for his one-time faithful servant God himself will in the end be sorry and find he has gone too far (21b).

That Job should not only feel neglected by God, but express his feeling publicly is not without parallel in the Bible. Sometimes to 'get it off one's chest' can be an emotional help, and even an expression of underlying trust in God. Jeremiah (20:7–18) provides one example. He expected to be heard, perhaps to be rebuked, and that brought God somehow closer to him. On the cross, Jesus cried 'why have you forsaken me?' (Mark 15:34, echoing Ps. 22:1) and to both Jesus and the Psalmist that cry resulted in new confidence (Luke 23:43, 46; Ps. 22:22–31). So it can be in our experience too.

THOUGHT: 'Jesus offered up prayers and supplications, with loud cries and tears . . . and he was heard for his godly fear' (Heb. 5:7).

Questions for further study and discussion on chapters 1–7

1. What difference does the Prologue in heaven make to the way we might view our Christian living?

2. In what ways is it helpful to study the role of Satan in our world?

3. What just cause has Job for complaint?

4. What are the perils of desiring to teach others about God (see notes on Job 4)?

5. Say why you think Eliphaz is right or wrong.

6. Why should Job not have taken his own life?

7. What would you do if a friend of yours were in a similar position to Job?

8. Discuss practical ways in which members of your Christian community are 'actually living as bearers of God's love in his world' (see notes on chapter 6). Can this be only done at a local level?

8 The justice of God

The second of Job's friends to speak is Bildad. In a comparatively brief speech he begins well by reminding Job that his complaint against God ought not to have been uttered, and that the angry ravings of a desperate man do not amount to good theology (2, 3). But his commendable desire to vindicate God leads him into an attempt to explain Job's sufferings to him, and thus he makes the same error as Eliphaz. God is infinitely greater than human explanations can ever describe. Bildad assumes Job's children (4) or Job himself (5, 6) must have sinned. He advises prayer as a means to even greater prosperity than before (5, 7).

Bildad's problem is created for him by his commitment to traditional theological views (8–10). He is so sure of the truth of the traditions he has received about God, that he makes the mistake of supposing them to be complete, with nothing more to be added. He may know his theology, but he lacks imagination. See, for another such error, Matthew 22:29. We, too, can make the same mistake.

A parable follows, to illustrate Bildad's point (11–19). A godless man, like a plant with no moisture, can only perish. It lives on rocky soil (17), and is exposed to the sun's heat (16), but, lacking moisture, will die, only to be succeeded by other equally short-lived plants. The man without God experiences similar impermanence and destitution, and is soon forgotten. The application to Job is obvious. For a New Testament use of this parable see Matthew 13:3–9. Bildad concludes (20–22) by hinting again at the happy future in store for Job if only he will get right with God.

The phrase used in verse 5, 'seek God', comes, after the Jewish exile in Babylon, to mean to pray in penitence (see Isa. 55:6–9). Job, like the exiles, could not seek God in the traditional way by worshipping at the true sanctuary, Jerusalem (see Amos 5:4–6).

TO THINK OVER: 'He advises prayer as a means to even greater prosperity before' – how may we be guilty of misusing prayer?

9 How can we be right with God?

Here and in chapter 10 Bildad receives an extended reply from a very perplexed Job. Verse 2 puts the question thoughtful people have asked in every age: if God does punish sin, how can a sinner escape his condemnation? Though the world had to wait for the Christian gospel to hear God's answer (2 Cor. 5:21), there have always been those in every age and continent whose refusal to despair, and whose trust in God for forgiveness, have brought them hope of salvation (see Rom. 2:12–16; 4:5). Job exhibits here a healthy respect for God's wisdom, and for his majestic power. He echoes the prophets (8, 9, compare Amos. 5:8, 9) and the psalms (10, compare Ps. 139:17, 18), but only to complain that his own case appears to be the exception: God doesn't care about Job (11), and no one can make him (12).

In such despair the desire to face God, and have it out with him in person, is understandable (13–24). But here is another insoluble problem. If God is omnipotent, how can man prevail against him? And if God is wise and just, what case can one make to persuade him of one's innocence? How, indeed, can he be summoned (16)? Job can only conclude that such a God is indifferent to good and evil alike (22), and worse, that he mocks those who fall into disaster (23). Perhaps (24, last phrase) he is not even in control, but there is instead a malignant power against whom God himself is impotent. See also Ecclesiates 7:13, where another wisdom writer allows himself to despair of God's work.

In verses 25–35 Job recapitulates his complaint, recognising that he cannot have many days to live (29); that nothing he can do will avail to clear his name (29–31); that he is in any case so terrified of this silent God that he could not cope with having to present his case to him (32–35); and complaining that there is no one who can mediate for him, since God is greater than man (32, 33). The New Testament knows otherwise (1 John 2:1, 2; 1 Tim. 2:5) but that is no reason for us not to share in and sympathise with the grief of those who do not.

10 A Creator who doesn't care

Though Job knows it is wrong, he persists in his foolish words (1), in the hope that at least this will attract God's attention to his case (2). We can only sympathise for this is an easily recognisable sign of impending panic. God is accused of cruelty and bias in favour of evil men (3). He is heartless, unaware of how things are for mere men (4, 5). He is unjust (6, 7), for he assumes Job is sinful when he is not, and treats him accordingly. He is indeed a creator, but one who has only given life and health in order to torment his creatures by taking them away (8–13, compare Ps. 139:13–16). It is noteworthy that many times Job echoes traditional Hebrew teaching about God, only to reject it as inadequate to his circumstances. God's disposition towards him is entirely malignant no matter what Job does (14–17). It's all too much to bear.

Job's only recourse is, once again, to bemoan his birth (see ch. 3). The grave, and the dark place where departed spirits are gathered together in shadowy half-life, knowing neither joy nor sorrow, pleasure nor pain, are preferable to life, with its injustice and sickness. The Hebrews in general had no consistent belief in personal and physical resurrection, and the pictures the Old Testament contains of Hades, of Sheol as it was called, are gloomy (21, 22, see also Isa. 14:9–11). The refusal Job shows in these chapters to let go of life, and of belief in God, illustrates how important life was to those for whom death held no prospect of God's nearer presence (see Ps. 88:3–12) or of richer life (see Heb. 2:14, 15).

FOR PRAISE AND THANKSGIVING: 'But if we have died with Christ, we believe that we shall also live with him. For we know that Christ being raised from the dead will never die again; death no longer has dominion over him' (Rom. 6:8, 9).

11;12 Head knowledge and heart knowledge

Chapter 11: Zophar has not spoken before. In this cycle of speeches he is the last to speak. Beginning like Bildad, he rebukes Job's many words (see Eccl. 10:12–14), and then begins to criticise Job's position. To Job's protestation of innocence Zophar simply offers denial (4, 5): like both his colleagues, he is persuaded that God does not visit the godly with calamity. God's wisdom is unsearchable (5–9) – a point the full significance of which Zophar has entirely missed – and he does not suffer foolish men to thwart his purposes (10). Hence there follows yet another appeal to 'set your heart aright' (13) and repent (14), with the usual impressive list of ensuing blessings (15–19). Zophar might have made a good evangelist for he sticks closely to the few things he knows about God, and presents them well, but as a pastor he has nothing to offer but platitudes which are off the point. Even his teaching about the fate of the wicked lacks sensitivity under the circumstances (20).

Chapter 12: Job senses this, and is short with him (1–3). He is hurt because God has made a fool of him by this apparent connivance in the triumph of evil. He shares the Psalmist's sense of having been deceived (4–6, compare Ps. 73:13). He is, however, in no doubt about God's power to control his life (7–10). The Lord of nature must also be Lord of man's affairs. If old men are wise (12), then how wise must God be (13–25)! The most impressive thing about Job in all these chapters is the firm hold he keeps on the sovereignty of God over all things. Only in 9:24 so far has he even begun to query this. When suffering comes, as it must in a sinful world, nothing is gained by denying the truths about God that Paul believed to be self-evident (Rom. 1:19, 20). Only in a God who is completely wise, completely powerful and completely good can there be hope for our world. Jesus himself, in a moment of acute testing, perceived that (Matt. 4:8–10).

QUESTION: How do we relate the sovereignty of God to the events we see on the television news and to instances of personal tragedy around us?

13:1–22 A man speaks to his God

Job, sure now of the bankruptcy of his friends' arguments, and convinced they are not more spiritually mature than he (1, 2), considers that he might himself address God. It is an awesome thought (20, 21), which had earlier filled him with dread (9:34) – a salutary reminder of God's majesty to those of us who are only too ready to address ourselves to him all unprepared. But now, given that he can get a word in edgeways (5), Job will speak, and risk the consequences (13). His friends had been painting over the facts with falsehoods (for instance, that God only sends disaster upon the wicked) and were useless to him in his need (4). They had presented prejudiced evidence, and in God's name, too (7, 8). All their theology is useless (12). Therefore they should fear God, for he requires no lies in his defence (10–12).

Job at least has the courage to be radical: if God does not like what he says, then Job is content to suffer the extreme penalty (13–15). But in his heart he is sure that God is good to the righteous so that if he begins his speech and lives, then there must be some other explanation of his agony (16). We are not to forget that in the midst of all this debate there lies a man still racked with pain, and tormented with the grief of bereavement and ruin. His friends must now listen (17), since they have not prevailed on him to be silent (19). He is sure he will receive a favourable judgement (18), and doesn't mind whether he or God speaks first in the hearing (22). God's intervention is to wait until the end of our drama, so it is Job upon whom this arduous task first falls. We must admire his courage, and commend his imagination. 'Nothing ventured, nothing gained.' He has nothing to lose, for his life is ebbing away, but much to gain in the form of new insights into what God might be like. Notice he does not for a moment consider that there might in fact be nothing for him to learn. His God is great enough to emerge with credit from this and any other test set him by a mere man.

QUESTION: Do we, like the three friends, cling to our existing ideas come what may, or are we, like Job, prepared to risk everything and trust all to God in the hope of making new discoveries of God?

13:23 – 14:22 Job's speech in God's court

Job's defence consists in putting some very important and basic questions to God (23–25). This is straight talking, and he wants straight answers. Assuming, for the sake of the occasion, that there is a written indictment against him (26), he objects that it refers to youthful indiscretions which are hardly to the point at this stage of his life. Furthermore, his sentence has preceded the trial (27), and he now feels much more deeply the sense of impermanence which he shares with all mankind (28).

This leads into a meditation on the nature of human experience, which might serve to soften the heart of his judge (14:1–22). Life is brief, and turbulent (1, 2), so it is unkind to make matters worse (3). Man is far from perfect, and it can't be helped (4). He doesn't live long (compare Gen. 6:3), so deserves to be left in peace by God (5, 6). A parable from nature is again used (7–22). Even a tree can come to life after being felled, and its stump will produce fresh growth. Isaiah predicted new life for the nation of Judah (Isa. 11:1–12); might the same not be possible for one man? Even after death might there not be hope of further life (13–15), and restoration of broken communion with God? Verse 15 contains a touching picture of the eager reunion envisaged. In the new life old things would have passed away, and all become new (16, 17, compare 2 Cor. 5:17). It is impressive to see how Job's faith in God's righteousness forces him to consider that even death itself might not be God's very last word on a man. But for Job it can only be a dream. He has no evidence, as Christians have, to support it. The grey realities of his present experience are forced back upon him (18–22), and the speech ends with a forlorn account of the inevitability of man's ageing and dying, the future all unknown, and only his pain real in his experience. It is precisely against this grim backdrop that the assurance we have of resurrection appears so glorious (1 Cor. 15:20–22).

THOUGHT: 'Death is swallowed up in victory.
O death, where is thy victory?
O death, where is thy sting?'
(1 Cor. 15:54, 55)

Questions for further study and discussion on chapters 8–14

1. How can our theology be marred by failure to use our imagination?

2. How would you answer the question in 9:2?

3. In a world made by God and full of suffering, can it be properly said that God is cruel, or helpless, or both?

4. There are some sensitive and intelligent people who have come to the conclusion that God is inconceivable and belief in him impossible. If you were with such a person, what would you say or do?

5. As a pastor Zophar 'has nothing to offer but platitudes which are off the point' (see notes on Job 11). What should a pastor offer when he is ministering to the sick, whether in body or mind?

6. On what ground do we believe we can speak to God? How awesome do we find the prospect to be (Job 13)?

7. How much can we learn about God from observing the world in which we live?

8. What are your reasons for believing in heaven? What do you think it is like? What difference does this belief make to your life (see notes on chapters 13 and 14)?

15 A worn out theme

A second cycle of speeches begins at this point as Job's friends make another attempt to explain his predicament to him. Eliphaz begins again, and this time is bolder in roundly accusing Job of sin. His words are mere wind (2, 3). He lacks that reverence for God which is wisdom's truest mark (4, compare 28:28), and his motives are deceitful (5). Job is charged with conceit (7), in setting himself higher than divine wisdom itself (see Prov. 8:25), and with claiming the sort of supernatural insights that the prophets had who listened in the inner councils of heaven (8, see 1 Kings 22:19-23; Jer. 23:18). His charge is ironic, for Eliphaz himself was not present in the heavenly councils of chapters 1 and 2. Eliphaz further claims the privilege of age (9, 10), and tells Job he is ungrateful (11). Repeating his earlier points, he asserts Job's guilt (14-16), and that of all creatures, suggesting that his sufferings are not unmerited (see 4:17-19; 5:1). He has added nothing new to the debate, beyond slandering the very person he is supposed to be consoling. As Christians nowadays we must be open to those who perceive the weakness of our arguments. We should not blame them when they refuse to be persuaded by our opinions. It takes a great gospel to provoke great conversions, and Eliphaz' philosophy is barren.

Warming to his played-out theme, Eliphaz tries rhetoric (what a contrast with 1 Thess. 1:5; 2:4, 13). Verses 17-35 offer Job exaggerated descriptions of the destiny and character of the wicked. Either they are patently untrue (e.g. 20, 23), or they are general and in no way relevant to Job. Eliphaz, unimaginative as ever, does not even consider that God might be keeping rewards beyond understanding for his suffering servant (compare 1 Pet. 5:10; Rom. 8:38, 39).

QUESTION: Are we ever justified in accusing others of sin?

16;17 Hope springs eternal

Chapter 16: Job's reply is ready, and is given with justifiable asperity (2, 3). But he does not allow himself the luxury of descending to the level of personal abuse, for from verse 6 he returns to his theme of the injustice of God. In another passage full of exaggerated metaphor he accuses God of unimaginable cruelty and of using human instruments as well as physical sickness as his means of assault upon Job's body and mind (6–16). And still he protests his innocence (17).

As Abel's blood called from the earth for vengeance (Gen. 4:10), so Job prays that his innocent blood will not drain unmarked into the earth (18). He has a witness in heaven (19) who will support his cause. Though his so-called friends ridicule him, Job is still sure God will maintain the ordinary standards of human justice and fair play (20, 21). But the time is coming when it will be too late (16:22–17:2).

Chapter 17: Job cannot believe that his friends are right. God must have had a reason for denying them understanding, and he cannot let them be vindicated. Only punishment is a fit reward for their betrayal (3–5). The Bible has a high view of the privilege of friendship (Prov. 18:24). A false friend is an unspeakable abomination. In the last part of this lament Job maintains his conviction that the distinction between right and wrong, wisdom and folly, good and evil has not been abolished, even if he cannot yet see how this is so (6–16). There is comfort neither in the words of others, nor in the prospect of his life's ambitions being destroyed by death. But hope dies hard, and the last verse is a question, not a statement.

FOR ENCOURAGEMENT: 'Yet the righteous holds to his way . . . ' (9) – if Job could do so how much more can we who know the truth of 2 Corinthians 12:9.

18 A salutary warning

There is in Bildad's words an element of gentle humour (2–4), in marked contrast to those of Eliphaz. He invites Job to consider that his verbosity is running away with him, and that his friends are not entirely bereft of sense. Job speaks as if the very order of nature should be restructured to accommodate his ideas.

But the gentleness of Bildad's approach does not betoken an improvement in his theology, for once again the remainder of the discourse presents a grim picture of the destiny of any man who does not know God (5–21). He lacks the resources to keep his lamp and fire fuelled, and his ways are always being thwarted and frustrated. He starts at any sudden noise, is hungry and beset by calamity. His skin is diseased (sickness was viewed by the Hebrews as the fingers of death clawing man before his time, see Ps. 88). The most awful of all the demons, whose delight is in tormenting man, has such a man dragged from his tent to face the terrors of darkness. His home becomes the property of others, and his substance comes to an end (contrast 2 Kings 19:30 with verse 16 here). Succeeded by neither fame nor descendants, his fate excites the horror and pity of men of all races. (For a similar picture see Isaiah 14, and compare Luke 16:19–31). Though, as with the words of Eliphaz, much of this is both general and exaggerated, its language reminds us of many of the sayings in the book of Proverbs, and provides a salutary warning of the end result of ignoring God. Nonetheless, true as much of it undoubtedly is, it does not say anything relevant about Job's situation.

QUESTION: Do we have an adequate understanding of the end result of ignoring God?

19 My Redeemer lives

To Job all this is no comfort, and once more he denies that he is a sinner. Or, if he is, it is not for any reason of which his friends or the public could have any knowledge (1–4). His cry of Violence! (the shout raised by one who had become a victim or witness of murder or robbery, and which should be heeded by the public) has gone unheeded, and it is God who is responsible. Even Job's relatives and friends are impervious to his plight (13–15), and his household and family care nothing for him (16, 17) – a feeling common, even if unjustified, among those who are deeply depressed. The respect which he should be given by the young is denied him, and replaced by abuse (18). One of the hardest things to bear, above even the loss of health and wealth, is the sense that those social relationships upon which we so often depend for our security and mental health have ceased to operate, and we are alone and unloved.

In a passage notoriously hard to translate (23–29), Job expresses a further conviction. He longs that his words might be inscribed for posterity, believing that, some time in the future there would be one who would take his part, and have the last word in the divine court. Job probably sees this happening after his death (for before death he could conduct his own defence). Furthermore Job expects to witness this in person (26b–27). He thus implies that the need for God to be seen to be just, and the justifier of those who trust him (Rom. 3:26), will actually override the effect of the curse in Genesis 3:17–19, and result in a life after death (whether physical or not is not stated). This, if Job's words are correctly understood, represents a triumph of faith almost unique (though see Dan. 12:2 and Isa. 26:19) in the Old Testament and is a continuation of the idea first aired in 14:7–17. That such ideas are commonplace in the New Testament, because of the resurrection of Jesus, should not prevent us marvelling at Job's intellectual and spiritual courage here. Who the Redeemer of verse 25 actually is, is a secret that has to wait for its time.

20;21 How to miss the point

Chapter 20: Zophar, taking his turn, fails to pay much attention to Job's theological *tour de force*. He makes the mistake of being too quick to speak (2, 3, compare Jas. 1:19), and shows he hasn't really been listening. Yet again we are treated to a monologue on the subject of the fate of the wicked (4–19), and from it learn no more than we did from Bildad. It is to the credit of Job's friends that they have grasped so clearly the truth that evil will not go unpunished, and have observed so perceptively the dissatisfaction of the self-centred. But their variations are on one theme, and the theme is from the wrong symphony.

Chapter 21: Job, too, is unable to sustain his previous standard of debate. But he does introduce a healthy note of sceptical protest (7–13). It is patently untrue to say the wicked have a bad time, when the evidence is that so many get away with it. The author of Psalm 73 had the same problem, and Ecclesiastes is tempted by it to doubt whether being righteous is that important (Eccl. 3:16, 17; 7:15–18). Job's picture of the influence of such men, their large families and farms, houses and parties, and eventual stately and decorous funerals is one which others have drawn down the ages. But the problem of evil cannot be resolved merely by bewailing the wickedness of the wealthy; envy is itself wrong (Ps. 37:1, 7, 8). The destiny of both poor and rich is alike (26), and there is little point in equating them with the just and the unjust (27–34). The problem of evil must be resolved at a deeper level than that.

Notes for further study and discussion on chapters 15–21

1. Is it enough, in Christian apologetic, to reproduce arguments we believe, but don't really understand?

2. What do you think was at the heart of the failure of Job's friends?

3. What would you say is the difference in being friends with someone, and being friendly with someone (see notes on Job 16; 17)? In what ways do people today trivialise and cheapen the friendship of Christ (compare John 15:14, 15)?

4. For an exercise in listening, divide into pairs. Let one person speak for two minutes, and the other listen without interruption. Then let the one listening try to repeat as accurately as possible to his partner what he has just heard. Then reverse the roles. What have you learnt from this?

5. Is Job's conviction that he will eventually be vindicated, even if only after death, irrational? In what ways does it contradict our knowledge of God, and in what ways confirm it?

6. What in fact would you say to someone who believes that to lead an amoral or immoral life is to get a better bargain than a moral person gets?

7. On what grounds can you say, 'I know that my Redeemer lives'?

8. One of our hymns has a verse which goes:
> 'If our love were but more simple
> We should take him at his word,
> And our lives would be all sunshine
> In the sweetness of our Lord.'

Do you agree with these words?

22 Repentance and faith

The third cycle of speeches now begins, but is probably incomplete. Job replies to Eliphaz (chs. 23;24), but Bildad's speech is much abbreviated (25), and Job replies three times (26, 27, 28, 29–31). Since Zophar's turn is unrecorded, it may be that his speech has been lost between chapters 26 and 27, or 28 and 29, or else that some of the words attributed to Job once belonged to Zophar's last speech. Chapter 28, with its serene and measured assertions about the immutable wisdom of God, has been thought by some to be an interpolation by the book's editor into the otherwise stormy speech sequences, to remind readers of what the truth about God really is. Certainly that chapter, as we shall see, represents a very different attitude to God from Job's usual one.

A résumé of the arguments may therefore help at this point. In the first cycle Eliphaz tells of God's moral purity, and Job retorts that nonetheless God has been cruel to him. Bildad asserts God's justice, and Job complains he hasn't had a hearing. Zophar reaffirms God's wisdom, but Job would like to have it out with God in person. In the second cycle Eliphaz repeats his first point, and adds that God punishes evil men, to which Job says that God seems to include him, the innocent, in his punishment. Bildad adds nothing to his first position, and Job retorts that God will take his part at the end. Zophar gently reminds Job that the wicked do not prosper ultimately, but Job's reply is that the evidence for such faith is lacking.

Eliphaz' final argument, here in chapter 22, consists of a detailed speculation about what Job's crime must be (1–11), and a reminder of God's inscrutability (12–14). He adds that the wicked do not, despite appearances, get away with it (15–20), so Job's best way is to 'return to the Almighty' (21–30), so as to receive his blessing. This last part of his discourse is a magnificent statement of the nature and consequences of repentance and faith (with verse 29 compare 1 Pet. 5:5). He is still, however, blinded by his erroneous premise that Job is guilty of a crime against God.

23 Terror of God

Still Job wants to stand at God's tribunal (1–7); there we all shall stand one day (2 Cor. 5:10). The New Testament echoes the Old in asserting that all have sinned (Ps. 14:1–3; Rom. 3:23). Job, however, knows that his blameless life merits no treatment such as God has meted out to him, for compared with others he is righteous (see Phil. 3:6). Job believes that if God is just, he must be seen to be just. If he is wrong he wants to be told so by God himself. Job's insistence on this is noble and courageous. The problem is that God is invisible. How then can he be found and addressed (8, 9)? Part of the solution is that God finds us (10), which is both good and bad.

Some of the ways in which God finds us are recorded elsewhere in the Bible. For Daniel it was in dreams (Dan. 7) for Jeremiah in an everyday occurrence (Jer. 18:1–6), for Isaiah it was at worship (Isa. 6). For Paul in a journey (Acts 9) and for Peter and his brother Andrew at work (Mark 1:16–18). What is important is not the way God meets us, but that when we recognise him we should respond appropriately. But this was Job's problem – what might he say? He was afraid (15). Adam's instinct in hiding from God was in part sound (Gen. 3:8–10), for if one is a sinner to have dealings with God is a terrible thing (Heb. 10:31), even though he is also full of compassion and kindness (see Exod. 34:6, 7). Job knows the terror of God (13–17), and is only partly reassured by recalling his own innocence (10–12). Not until the New Testament was this awful dilemma ever resolved (see Rom. 5:6–11).

THOUGHT: 'I revealed myself to those who did not ask for me;
I was found by those who did not seek me.
To a nation that did not call on my name
I said, "Here am I, here am I".'
(Isaiah 65:1)

24 God's indifference to evil men

Job's protest now assumes a modern and universal ring. God, he says, ought to be answerable to man for the terrible things that happen in his world (1). The chapter contains a moving account, hardly bettered by the literature of modern social concern, of the evil way in which society works in every age (2–25). Its features are an apparent silence from God (1, 12c), robbery (2, 14c), murder (14), adultery (15), abuse of power (3, 4), acute hunger and poverty (5–12), torture (17), oppression of those unable to help themselves (21). Despite assertions by the pious that for the wicked there is no future (18–20), there is room for the awful suspicion that God connives at it all (22, 23), even though wicked men do not live for ever (24). The onus of proof lies upon those who assert otherwise (25). The text of the chapter is uncertain, and its style uneven (see RSV notes, brackets in verse 9, and prefixed 'You say' in verse 18), but it is clear enough to make Job's point, and his point is valid.

It is noteworthy that Job has here risen above personal concern for his own fate, to caring deeply about the fate of others, thus, incidentally, giving the lie to Eliphaz' accusations in 22:2–11. When one can see one's own griefs as part of the total grief of the human race, then only are they seen in true perspective, and then only is there hope that their causes can be rectified, whether by men or by God. Job's social conscience was not atrophied (see 29:12–17).

QUESTION: How sensitive are we to the grief and pain of a creation 'groaning in travail' (Rom. 8:22)? Do we 'groan inwardly' as we long not simply for the consummation of our own individual salvation but for the restoration of the entire created order?

25;26 The Lord of nature

Chapter 25: Bildad's reply is brief, but to the point. Job doubts God's sovereign goodness, but God's greatness ought not to be impugned. He is an awesome God, and powerful above all other so-called powers (the natural sense of 2b). His armies (3) are the stars of heaven (compare Judg. 5:20; Ps. 147:4), and men in comparison are sinful (4) and weak (6). Even the heavenly bodies are nothing in comparison with the greatness of their Creator. The implication of this is that Job ought not to be criticising the wisdom or power of God in his dealings with men.

Chapter 26: Job reacts with sarcasm (2–4). Bildad's point is both obvious and well-known, and Job has never denied the greatness of the Creator. It is precisely because he accepts that fact that a theological problem is raised for him by the pains that he and others have to endure. There is no 'problem of evil' for those who believe in no God, or if there is, it is insecurely rooted in the conviction that goodness *ought* to be the rule amongst men. But Job now shows himself quite clear about God's greatness (5–14). God is Lord of the underworld (5, 6), the earth (7), the clouds (8), the moon (9), light and darkness (10 – for the waters compare Gen. 1:6–8), heaven (11) and even of cosmic powers opposed to him (12, 13). Verses 12, 13 refer to an old international myth that at the creation God fought and destroyed a great sea-monster, and imprisoned her beneath the waters: see Job 38:8–11, Psalm 74:12–17, Isaiah 27:1; 51:9–10, etc. And even all of this is like the rustle of his robes: the full reality has yet to be revealed! See Psalm 139:17, 18.

THOUGHT: Because Christians believe in an omnipotent, sovereign God, they should have a deeper awareness of, and sensitivity to, the problems raised by the pain and suffering of humanity.

27 Fighting against God

It has been argued that verses 7–23 might come better from the lips of Zophar than of Job. Alternatively, Job is beginning to concede or use some of his friend's arguments. Either way, he begins (1–6) by reaffirming his own integrity, honesty and righteousness. He denies that he will ever concede that they are right (5).

Verses 7–23 are an imprecation against his enemies, and express Job's hope that their fate will conform to the pattern by now familiar from the speeches of his friends, especially those of the second cycle. Such anger is understandable, even if not entirely justifiable (see Matt. 5:43–48). Job takes some delight in turning his friends' argument against them (11, 12). The children of the opponents of God are destined for violent death or hunger, or for fatal disease. Their riches will be dispersed, their homes destroyed, and their emotional security dissipated by the sudden onslaught of indescribable terrors and disasters. If Zophar is the speaker, he is addressing all the participants in the debate (11, 12), and reasserting their thesis in stronger terms. If it is Job (as seems more likely), then he is reviewing their argument, but only to show them that they will be its victims, because it is they, not he, who have been found fighting against God (compare Acts 5:38, 39) – an idea which they have not yet shown sufficient humility to entertain. The friends from this point fade into the background of the debate, their arguments found wanting, and lacking charity and humility. They are even ignored by God in his own address (chapters 38–42), and from now until chapter 31 Job alone continues the debate.

TO THINK OVER: 'You might even be found opposing God!' (Acts 5:39).

28 'Where can wisdom be found?'

In the world of the ancient Near East the nature of wisdom was often a subject for debate. Wisdom might be found encapsulated in short, memorable proverbs, or at greater length in fables and disputes promoted by those who had ideas they wished to disseminate. Some of the extant literature approaches the style of philosophical tracts, but in the Hebrew scriptures the word wisdom usually has practical and moral, rather than philosophical, overtones. The constant contribution of the Old Testament to this debate is the reiterated assertion that the 'fear of the Lord' (that is, the religion of Yahweh) is wisdom, and that a wise man will follow the moral principles which ensue. The climax of chapter 28 constitutes such an assertion.

As is characteristic of 'wisdom' literature, the chapter examines the world of human achievement (1–11) and of natural things (12–19) to see whether wisdom is to be found in them. Even death, here personified, and the inhabitants of the underworld, who might well be expected to know more of the truth about God and man, can tell us little. Wisdom is not hidden in some inaccessible earthly location (7, 8). God alone, he who made all things and from whom nothing is concealed, knows where it is to be found. It is found only in reverence for the God of Israel, and in obedience to his moral laws (23–28). This fact, moreover, God has revealed to man.

On Job's lips this meditation must mean that in his search for enlightenment about his personal predicament he is rejecting the systematic theology and the philosophical dogmatism of his friends. Instead he clings to one fact which, despite his suffering, has won his firm allegiance. His moral character, stemming as it does from his reverence for God, can be charged with neither sin nor folly. He has done the right thing, and the rest is up to God.

THOUGHT: As Christians we can add a further dimension to the concept of God's wisdom: ' . . . Christ crucified. . . the power of God and the wisdom of God' (1 Cor. 1:23, 24).

29 Wisdom in practice

The evidence that Job himself is no stranger to the ways of wisdom, despite the opinions of his friends, is now supplied from the first verse to the last of this chapter. He looks back nostalgically to his younger and stronger days (autumn [4] is when the rains come, grass grows again after the drought, and sap is in the trees – a picture of youth and strength rather than frailty and decay), and recalls how he was loved for his generosity and philanthropy. He can remember his prosperity (7) and the respect in which he was held by the citizenry of his town as he fulfilled his duties as a magistrate (7–10). His judgements were fair, and he cared about the causes of the poor, the orphaned and the widowed as the law and the prophets demanded (compare Exod. 22:21–24; Deut. 10:17, 18; Jer. 5:28; Jas. 1:27). Like Barnabas (on whose feast day Job 29 is traditionally read, see Acts 4:36) Job was a 'son of encouragement' (the word might also mean consolation), and used his influence to break the power of the ungodly, as God does (22:29, Luke 1:51–53). Not only his official judgements, but also his private counsel (21–25) were eagerly sought and respected. Job clearly had the qualities that make a leader of men, and was accepted as such by his contemporaries. In all this he is certainly a model for all who seek to show the love of God in their lives and to obey what Jesus taught us are the greatest commands of the law (Matt. 22:34–40).

FOR MEDITATION AND ACTION: Read Psalm 146 as an example of God's priorities. Pledge yourself to care more and do more for the oppressed and underprivileged of the world. Set yourself realistic goals and plan to meet them.

30 Changed circumstances

Now, however, everything has altered. Job, who once was held in so high esteem by the elders of his city, is mocked and stared at by beggars, the simple-minded, the unemployable and refugees from justice (1–8). Even their distressed condition is better than his, and they feel sufficiently safe in their comparative security to express their disgust and contempt for one who was once their champion (9–11). What they have to say to him only makes matters worse (12–15), and there is neither comfort nor gratitude from that source. How much worse must it have been for Jesus on the cross, reviled by those he was dying to save (Matt. 27:27–50).

His personal sickness and pain were also his enemies (16–23), and at night his suffering became unendurable, with nothing and no one to distract him. God had done it, and done it thoroughly. The Almighty was indeed with him now (see 29:4, 5), but as tormentor, not as friend (19). Contrast, in the New Testament, John 16:32b with Mark 15:34. Death alone, Job thought, could terminate his pain. But he was reckoning without God, whose inscrutable purpose had not yet become plain and who could bring joy to birth through sorrow and pain. Verses 24–31 further express his sickness (28, 30), confusion (24–27) and loneliness (29, 31: for 'ostrich', RSV, read with NEB 'desert owl'). Even genuine compassion for the wretched is no guarantee against the onset of calamity in one's own life (25), nor of support from others when it comes.

THOUGHT: 'When he was reviled, he did not revile in return; when he suffered he did not threaten: but he trusted to him who judges justly' (1 Pet. 2:23).

31 The end of Job's complaint

In conclusion, Job searches his life and conscience for evidence of a crime that might have deserved such a punishment as his. We can today, even given our different customs, laws and circumstances, learn from his sense of right and wrong. He was a married man, so how could he have contemplated adultery (1, compare Matt. 5:28)? God's sentence might then have been just (2–4). But he had vowed to forswear sexual lust. Have we?

Has he been dishonest, in word or deed (5–8)? In his work as a magistrate, in paying his employees, in trade or in gossip he knew the value of honesty. The dishonest deserve disaster.

Has he slept with another man's wife (9–12)? That would be an offence against her, her husband, his wife, his marriage and his God. Its punishment belongs to this world's courts, and to the realm beyond the grave.

Has he been unjust in his dealings with his employees (13–15)? God takes the part of the underdog, so it is with God he would have to reckon. But as it is, he knows that all men are created equal in God's sight.

Has he neglected his responsibilities to the underprivileged (16–23)? He shared his meals, and never ate alone, distributed clothing and helped those who lacked a protector. He never used threats or influence to secure a false verdict in court. To fail in these spheres is to court disaster from God. Furthermore he denies financial corruption (how many today can do that?), and idolatry. There is only one God, and no power in the constellations or the zodiac (24–28). His concern for others has been genuine, and no indictment on such counts can be produced against him (29–37), for it would be easy to refute. His lands were bought and paid for (38–40), and not unjustly acquired. Can we say the same of our possessions?

FOR PRAYER: We may care to use Psalm 139:23, 24.

Questions for further study and discussion on chapters 22–31

1. What would you say to someone who said to you, 'How can God be found and addressed?' (see notes on Job 23)?

2. What does wisdom really mean, and how is it related to knowledge? Can one who does not believe in God be wise?

3. What do you understand by 'the fear of God'?

4. What verdict must be passed on us, judged by the standards of Job 31? What can we do to change our ways?

5. Are we, like Job (chapter 29), useful and respected members of our community? If not, why not? When should we care about earning the respect of others (compare 1 Tim. 3:1–7)?

6. Why are some people today criticised and scorned (chapter 30)? Pray for any such people you know.

7. How do we react to criticism, gloating or misunderstanding from other people?

8. Job vows never to deny the truth (27:4, 5). Is this a vow all Christians should make and live by? Are there times when it is acceptable to tell lies, for example, if one is involved in highly confidential work?

32 The voice of youth

Of Elihu, the next speaker, we hear nothing elsewhere in this book, or, for that matter, in the Bible. He may have been a Hebrew (for Buz, v. 2, see Gen. 22:21), but perhaps he is simply one of the crowd who are present to witness this debate. He is ignored in the final speeches and epilogue, but has a substantial contribution to make (in terms of length) to the discussion. It may be that the final editor of Job added these speeches to an earlier text to emphasise points he felt were too little heeded in the main debate. No text exists, though, in which these chapters (32–37) are absent.

Properly, as befits a young man, Elihu has kept silent so far, out of respect for age and greater wisdom (6, 7). However, the failure of Job's friends to answer Job angers him (3), as does Job's resolute conviction that his sufferings are undeserved (2). Because the friends have given up (13, 14), Elihu has decided to add his own points to their speeches, and he confesses he is bursting to interrupt (15–22). He will come straight out with his opinions, for he lacks the capacity to be reticent, polite or cautious. His is the voice of callow youth, governed as much by emotion as by reason. The force of his convictions has blinded him to the fact that he is dealing both with a man in deep physical and spiritual need, and with a matter the origin and significance of which (chs. 1;2) he has entirely missed. That in the dénouement of chapters 38–42 he is ignored is not surprising, but given the unsatisfactory state of the debate at this point he deserves a hearing. God does not deny wisdom to the young (8, 9, compare 1 Tim. 4:12), and there are times when young people demonstrate an intellectual vigour, independence and honesty which their elders lack, as well as a lively sense of compassion for the helpless.

QUESTION: Would Elihu get a hearing in our churches today?

33 'I will teach you wisdom'

Elihu at last gets to the point, and protests his sincerity (1–3). Acknowledging his creaturely dependence on God (4), he challenges Job to listen (5–7), as one mortal man to another. In this at least he is humble, and a pattern for all who seek to impart spiritual truth to others.

Job's argument is summarised (8–11) as an assertion that God has treated him badly, but that this cruelty is unmerited, for Job is guiltless. In reply, Elihu points out that God has many ways of speaking to men (12–14), for example in dreams used as warnings (15–18), or by pain (19–28), as may be the case with Job. One should not rule out any experience as a means by which God may choose to rebuke, warn, teach, encourage or restrain his creatures. Sickness is used, says Elihu, to bring sinners to repentance (27, 28), which may happen as a result of the intercession of an angelic power (23–25) who can offer a ransom for the sufferer so that he is restored to a penitent frame of mind and to health ('thousand' in v. 23 is a likely reference to the heavenly court, compare 1 Kings 22:19–22; Dan. 7:10; Rev. 5:11). A less likely interpretation would be to see the 'angel' as a human messenger from God who would interpret Job's predicament. Either way Elihu is sure he can help Job to see his plight for what it really is. If Job is innocent he should now answer, for Elihu wants only his righteousness (32). If guilty, then Job should keep quiet so that Elihu can instruct him (33) and reverse his perilous approach to death (22, 30).

Elihu's speech has two characteristics from which we can learn lessons. He exhibits conceit (see especially v. 33), which rather spoils his humble start, but also a powerful mastery of the theological arguments available to him. While Christians can emulate the latter, the former has no place in pastoral ministry. Elihu's words in verses 23–25 contain a moving anticipation of the ransom theology of the New Testament (see Mark 10:45; 1 Tim. 2:6 and Tit. 2:14): contrast Ps. 49:7, 8 (see RSV footnote).

QUESTION: Should we accept all experiences as an opportunity to learn?

34 An appeal to the audience

It is to Job's three friends that Elihu now addresses himself (2), inviting their approbation (3). Job, he tells them, must be an evil man, for he claims to be sinless, and sees no profit in a piety which he maintains brings only grief (5–9). Such blasphemy is unthinkable, for it implies that God is immoral, and it contradicts the dogma that God treats men as they deserve (see Rom. 2:6). It is the prerogative of the Creator, who is answerable to no higher authority, to destroy life as well as to give it (10–15). This is true enough in principle, but untrue to the revealed character of God, who has a strong bias towards saving his sinful creatures (Dan. 9:9), and who permits troubles for other than punitive reasons. Elihu appeals, rightly, to the fact that God is both just and impartial (16–20, compare Gen. 18:25), and points out that sudden death comes indiscriminately to all men. Thus Job should not suppose that he can come before God's judgement seat at a time of his own choosing (23, compare 24:1).

Little sense can be made of the text of verses 29–33 in its present state, but it is clear from verses 34–37 that Elihu concludes as he began by appealing to the discerning amongst his listeners to vindicate his thesis and reprove Job as an impious and proud sinner. Elihu has done nothing to prove his argument, and falls short on knowledge of the case, on compassion and on logic – he limits the possible reasons for God's deed. His bombastic self-esteem is thus unjustified, but it is clear he proposes to continue!

REMEMBER: Any judgement based on a partial knowledge of the facts is almost certain to be inaccurate and unhelpful.

35:1–36:23 Reasons for unanswered prayer

Chapter 35: Had Job really been thinking, as Elihu now supposes (1–3), that the only point of piety is the immediate advantages piety brings, then his religion would be no better than the Accuser had declared it to be in 1:9–11. True faith in God is rooted, not in his rewards, but in his beauty. Elihu tries to say something of this (4–8): God is high and exalted, and cannot be concerned with the petty presents men may offer him of their little acts of righteousness, nor yet with their fits of pique. Men wish to use him when they are in trouble (9), but not from motives of gratitude or love (10–11). Their concerns are with themselves, and so they fail to have any genuine relationship with God (12, 13). Job, says Elihu, is like that: he is pouring out verbiage, but only as an instinctive cry of pain in his plight, not out of reverence for God (14–16). Thus Elihu anticipates in part God's own accusation in 38:2.

Chapter 36: Fortified in his conviction that he is right by this long speech, Elihu's conceit grows (1–4). His role as extoller of God's greatness has made him seem important in his own eyes – a danger from which many Christian public speakers appear not to be immune. God *does* punish the guilty, Elihu tells us, and even explains their faults to them, to provide a chance of repentance (5–12). Job himself had been tempted by God out of a situation of need into prosperity and rewarded with wealth (15, 16) – information not supplied elsewhere in this book. But he is proving ungrateful, and his anger at God is inappropriate (17–23). It is not, however, without precedent, see Jeremiah 20:7–18.

THOUGHT: True faith in God is rooted, not in his rewards, but in his beauty.

36:24–37:24 The greatness of God

Chapter 36: At this point Elihu again begins to anticipate the later divine speeches. Verses 24–33 constitute a magnificent account of the way in which God reveals something of his greatness in natural phenomena – rain (27, 28) and clouds, thunder and lightning (29, 30) with which he both prospers and punishes nations everywhere (31). But Elihu is still blinkered by his ideas about divine retribution, so he can cynically and without evidence assert that natural disasters are necessarily caused by human sin (32, 33).

Chapter 37: To this traditional picture of God as one who is master of storm and tempest (compare Ps. 18:7–15; 2 Sam. 22:8–16) Elihu adds further evidence of God's greatness. Snow and rain, ice and whirlwind are also instruments of his purpose in administering justice (6–13). Job cannot pretend to such greatness (in point of fact he never has), so should not be so rash as to question such a God (14–20). Job's knowledge is as insignificant as his power to control nature (notice the question in Mark 4:41), and God is, in any case, too glorious and resplendent in majesty for men to see. That is why he is to be feared, and that is why he ignores the arrogance of conceited men (21–24).

Elihu's case is now made. He has not added much to that of Job's three friends, beyond further rebukes to Job, and further praise of God's greatness. Like them, he is caught up in the narrowness of his own inherited understanding of God, not allowing God to act beyond the confines of his theological system. As all the protagonists fall silent, unable to agree or understand, there is only one possible speaker left to tell us the truth about it all.

TO THINK OVER: What can we make of the apparent inconsistency of a man who claims to know all the answers and yet says: 'The Almighty – we cannot find him. . .'? Is there a challenge here for us?

38 God speaks

It is out of a sudden whirlwind that the God of storm and tempest speaks (1). Already hailed by Elihu as Lord of nature (chs. 36–37), and revealed to Moses in cloud and fire (Exod. 19:16–19), God at last appears, in response to Job's prayer (23:3–17). Thus at the same time he both vindicates Job's righteousness to the friends who accused Job of arrogance and sin, and reminds Job of the ancient Hebrew traditions about where God dwells (Ps. 104:3, 4). For a superb ancient hymn to Yahweh as God of mountain and storm see Habakkuk 3. Now it is God's turn to ask the questions, and they will require courage to hear (3). Job's speeches (the others are all ignored, for the problem is Job's not theirs: they didn't even get the question right, let alone the answers) were ill-informed, and produced, as it were, more heat than light (2).

Then, in language strongly reminiscent of some of the Psalms (is this deliberate?) and of Isaiah 40, God provides his own credentials (4–41). The speech is designed to show up Job's weakness and ignorance, and God's wisdom and greatness. The point is simple: all that is, God made. No creature can equal such wisdom, nor prevail against such might. To doubt God's wisdom, as Job had (9:21–24), or to query his power (9:24c), is folly.

The chapter, and those that follow, deserve to be read aloud. God is Creator, and the angels acknowledge it (4–7). He is Lord of the restless sea (8–11) and of day and night (12–21). Snow and rain are his to command (22–30); even the constellations (which some revered as gods, see also 30:26, 27) own his rule alone. The clouds, with their rain and lightning, are all the work of God's hands (34–38).

39 The Lord of nature

God's speech continues and turning now to the world of animal life
– in some ways even more marvellous and complex than the inanimate
creation (see also Psalm 104). Lions and ravens (38:39–41), wild goats,
asses and oxen (39:1–12) are described in all their beauty and strength.
There is a vibrant vitality in the natural order which had for the most
part been overlooked in the rather academic debate that has just con-
cluded. There is an element of humour here, too, which the earlier
discourses lack and which is a necessary part of any true appreciation
of God. See especially verses 13–18, of the ostrich! The picture of the
war-horse, and his eagerness for battle, must be unparalleled in literature of comparable antiquity (19–25). No less marvellous is the smooth
and high soaring of hawk and eagle, and their incredible powers of
sight in seeking their prey (26–30). The inaccessibility to man of the
eagle's eyrie reminds the hearer of human limitations. How can man,
then, seek out the mind of the almighty Creator, and comprehend his
ways?

WORSHIP: 'O the depth of the riches and wisdom and knowledge of
God! How unsearchable are his judgements and how inscrutable his
ways!
    "For who has known the mind of the Lord, or who has been his
    counsellor? Or who has given a gift to him that he might be
    repaid."
For from him and through him and to him are all things. To him be
glory for ever. Amen.' (Rom. 11:33–36)

40 All creatures great and small

Job is learning his lesson. When he had wanted to dispute with God he had not realised his presumption. Now he sees that he has no answers to God's questions (1–5). He knows he has said enough, possibly too much, and is content, even in his pain, to listen humbly to his Master's voice, and savour the majestic glory of his Creator's comforting presence. Of the terror he so dreaded (13:21) there is no sign. God will speak again, and in the same manner (6–9).

In rebuke to those who had earlier suggested that God is indifferent to the arrogance of great men, God reveals that he alone has the power to abase them (10–14). If Job can do it too, well and good! Then, moving from the lesser creatures of chapter 39, God draws the hearers' attention to the mightiest beasts they know (15–24). The first is Behemoth, probably the hippopotamus (though he is unknown in the Jordan, 23, and does not climb hills, 20. Nor is his tail quite as verse 17 suggests. An accurate identification is as yet impossible). His ponderous might should inspire awe (19), and who is there on earth who could catch him with a mere fishing line (24)? Foremost amongst God's creatures (19a), he too reveals God's might and skill.

QUESTION: How do we, in a modern scientific age, many of us living in large cities remote from the natural features and beasts God mentions, respond to these chapters?

41 Leviathan

The Hebrew Bible continues chapter 40 until verse 8 of this, but the division in the English versions makes better sense, for a new marvel is now described, Leviathan (for the name, see Isa. 27:1; Ps. 74:14; 104:26.) Originally a name given in the Ancient Near East to the mythical sea-monster, slain by God at creation, it became, as here and in Psalm 104, the name given to large aquatic beasts, such as the whale or the crocodile. In this chapter the latter is the more likely. This is the longest description of one creature in all the divine speeches, and the writer allows us to view his subject from many angles – a good way to look at any work of God.

Crocodiles are not good pets (1–5)! Nor are they bartered in town markets (6). Just try catching one (7–10a)! God alone is his master, and has neither creditors nor equals (10b–11). There is no respect in which man can lay claim to any part of God's world, for all was made by him and belongs to him. The appearance of the beast is formidable (12–25), and he is almost impenetrable to the hunter's usual puny armoury (26–29). His passage over land and sea leaves the observer in no doubt about his size and strength (30–32). He is peerless, and knows it (33–34).

Thus God concludes his object lesson on wisdom and power, lifting the whole debate on to a higher plane. Here it has to take itself less seriously, and make room for a larger vision of God.

QUESTION: Can we sometimes take ourselves, and our ideas, too seriously? What are the dangers of doing so?

42 Happily ever after

The first six verses of this chapter conclude the poetic dialogue, which began at Chapter 3. Job is now suitably chastened, and recognises that God's accusation (38:2) was fair (3). God is indeed omnipotent (2) and truly wise (3, 4). The fault lay in Job's small conception of God, whom he had tried to fit into his own world of reward and punishment, debate and vindication. The theophany, the vision of God, has changed all that (5), and at last he can see himself in true perspective (6a) and repent of his sin in belittling his God (6b). A translation recently suggested for 6b is 'and repent of dust and ashes', that is, cease from wallowing in self-pity in the garbage pile, and return to make something worthwhile out of the ruins of his former life and health (compare 2:8).

An epilogue (7–17) follows, in prose, and using similar vocabulary to that in chapters 1 and 2. Though no record is offered of Satan's reaction to Job's change of heart and constant reverence for God, the friends are rebuked for their error (7–9), and their sin has to be atoned for by sacrifice and prayer from Job himself. Elihu is unmentioned. Thereafter Job's prosperity is restored to him, and multiplied (10). Relatives (remarkably absent earlier) come to congratulate him, and give him presents (11). His property increases, and he has more children (12–15), the girls in particular being noted beauties. Job himself is blessed with an unusually long life (16, compare Gen. 6:3; Ps. 90:9, 10; Isa. 65:20), and sees his grandchildren (perhaps great-grand-children). He dies at length at a great age, 140 years after these events. The verdict of the New Testament can be seen in James 5:10, 11: Job was patient, but even better, God was merciful. Patient endurance of undeserved suffering resulted in Jesus' case in an even greater demonstration of mercy (Rom. 5:15–21; Phil. 2:5–11). Are we capable of such faith, obedience and endurance?

Questions for further study and discussion on chapters 32–42

1. What limitations should be ascribed to the opinions and advice of the young?

2. What are the ways God uses to speak to men today (see notes on chapter 33)?

3. Is Elihu's opinion about the reasons for unanswered prayer both true and adequate (compare 35:9–16)?

4. What use ought Christians to make of traditional scriptural and liturgical material in pastoral counselling and evangelism?

5. What can be learned from nature about God?

6. 'True faith in God is rooted, not in his rewards but in his beauty' (see notes on chapter 35). Discuss your views on this.

7. How is Job's problem resolved by the divine speeches in chapters 38–42?

8. Prepare a service of worship based on your study of this book.